A Division of Macmillan Computer Publishing
201 West 103rd St., Indianapolis, Indiana 46290 USA

 For information, address Que Corporation, 201 W. 103rd Street, Indianapolis, IN 46290. You can reach Que's direct sales line by calling 1-800-428-5331.

International Standard Book Number: 0-7897-0569-9
Library of Congress Catalog Card Number: 95-78879

97 96 95 3 2 1

Interpretation of the printing code: the rightmost number of the first series of numbers is the year of the book's printing; the rightmost number of the second series of numbers is the number of the book's printing. For example, a printing code of 95-1 shows that the first printing of the book occurred in 1995.

President and Publisher Roland Elgey

Publisher, Que New Technologies Stacy Hiquet

Publishing Director Brad R. Koch

Editorial Services Director Elizabeth Keaffaber

Managing Editor Sandy Doell

Director of Marketing Lynn E. Zingraf

Senior Series Editor Chris Nelson

Publishing Manager Tom Bennett

Acquisitions Editor Beverly M. Eppink

Product Director Mark Cierzniak

Production Editor Noelle Gasco

Assistant Product Marketing Manager Kim Margolius

Technical Editor Tobin Anthony

Technical Specialist Cari Ohm

Acquisitions Coordinator Ruth Slates

Operations Coordinator Patricia J. Brooks

Editorial Assistant Andrea Duvall

Book Designer Kim Scott

Cover Designer Dan Armstrong

Production Team Steve Adams, Angela D. Bannan, Chad Dressler, Joan Evan, Amy Gornik, Damon Jordan, Bob LaRoche, Julie Quinn, Bobbi Satterfield, Kelly Warner, Paul Wilson

Indexer Carol Sheehan

To my wife, Anita—see, I told you I'd finally take a vacation—and to my favorite author, Jesus Christ.

About the Author

Noel Estabrook is currently a faculty member of the College of Education at Michigan State University after having obtained degrees in Psychology, Education, and Instructional Technology. He is heavily involved in delivering Internet Training and technical support to educators, professionals, and laymen. He also runs his own training business part-time in addition to writing. Most recently, he has been involved in authoring on the Web and has coauthored Que's *Using UseNet Newgroups* and *Using FTP*. His e-mail address is **noele@msu.edu.**

Acknowledgment

To Beverly Eppink at Que—I finally have a book with just *my* name on it!

Contents

Introduction

The story goes that Henry Ford had just succeeded in getting the first auto assembly line up and running when, one day, the machine mysteriously quit working. Naturally, he called in the best engineer he could find to look at his machine.

Instead of looking closely at the machine, however, he simply walked from one end to the other—never touching, always looking. Finally, he walked back to the middle of the factory, took one last look at the machine, and then walked up to it, flipped open a panel, and pushed a large red button. The assembly line immediately roared back to life!

Naturally, Henry was ecstatic, "That's fantastic! I can't tell you how thankful I am. What do I owe you?"

The man replied matter-of-factly, "$10,000."

"$10,000?" Henry asked incredulously, "But it only took you five minutes and all you did was press a button!"

"That's right," said the expert, "but I knew *which* button to press."

The amount of information available on the Internet is mind-boggling, and growing faster than anyone can ever hope to keep up with. When tapping into this wealth of information, wouldn't it be great if you knew which button to press?

Well, you can, and it won't cost you $10,000, either. What you have in your hand is a storehouse of information and experience—experience that you can put to use right now. Welcome to the *10 Minute Guide to Netscape for the Mac.*

How To Use This Book

This book is divided into a series of lessons designed to show you all you need to know to use Netscape confidently. The first few lessons show you how to browse the World Wide Web with ease. The next few lessons help you use Netscape to keep track of where you've been and quickly go to places you want to go.

After that, you learn how to search for various people, places, and information on the Internet. Following that, you learn how to access non-Web resources, such as Gopher and FTP, using Netscape. The next group of lessons show you how to access images, audio, and movies to take full advantage of the multimedia nature of the Web. Finally, we show you how to customize Netscape so that it works just the way you want it to.

CONVENTIONS USED IN THIS BOOK

You'll find icons throughout this book to help you save time and learn important information fast:

Timesaver Tips These give you insider hints for using Netscape more efficiently.

Plain English These icons call your attention to definitions of new terms.

Panic Button Look to these icons for warnings and cautions about potential problem areas.

You'll also find common conventions for steps you will perform:

What you type	Things you type will appear in bold, color type.
Press Enter	Any keys you press or items you select with your mouse will appear in color type.
On-screen text	Any on-screen messages you will see will appear in bold type.
New terms	New terms will appear in italic.

TRADEMARKS

Screen reproductions in this book were created by means of the program Capture from Mainstay, Camarillo, CA.

Starting and Quitting Netscape

In this lesson, you learn how to start and quit Netscape. You also learn about the Netscape screen, the Netscape home page, and how to get online help.

Home Page A home page is merely the name given to a company, group, or organization's initial screen, or "page," on the World Wide Web. Individuals are also creating their own home pages more and more every day.

Starting Netscape

The first step in browsing the World Wide Web using Netscape is starting the program. Simply locate the **Netscape** icon and you're ready to go (see Figure 1.1). Many people choose to put all of their communications programs into one folder for easy access. You may want to do the same.

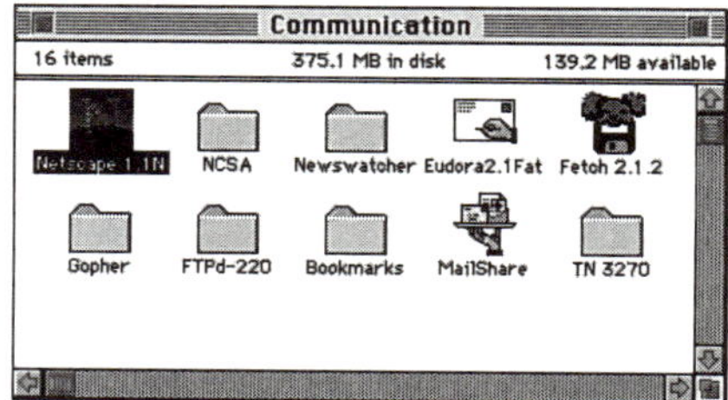

Figure 1.1 The Netscape icon in the Communication folder.

To start Netscape, simply double-click the Netscape icon. The program starts and displays Netscape's home page (see Figure 1.2).

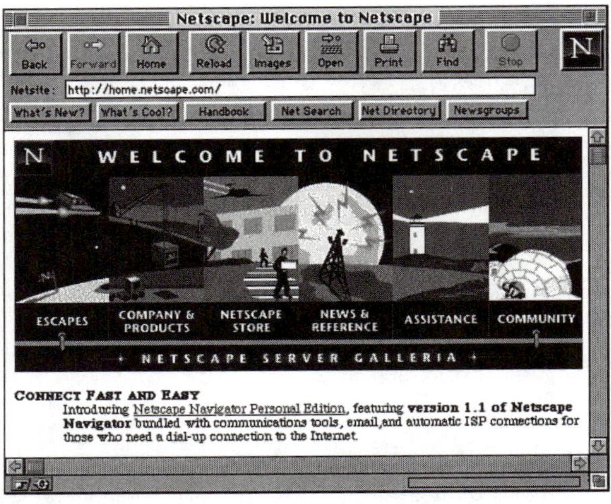

FIGURE 1.2 Netscape's home page.

Where's Netscape's Home Page? If you start Netscape and the Netscape home page is not displayed, it is possible your connection to the Internet has either been broken or may not be set up correctly.

It is also possible that Netscape's home page is just busy. Try to connect several times. If you still do not get it, check with your Internet provider to make sure you are properly connected.

The first time that you start Netscape, you're presented with a License Agreement to use the Software. Read this document carefully, and if you agree to it, click the Accept button.

UNDERSTANDING THE PARTS OF THE NETSCAPE SCREEN

Besides the usual features of most Macintosh applications—title bar, Close box, scroll bars, and so on—Netscape has its own unique set of screen features. Figure 1.3 highlights these unique features for you.

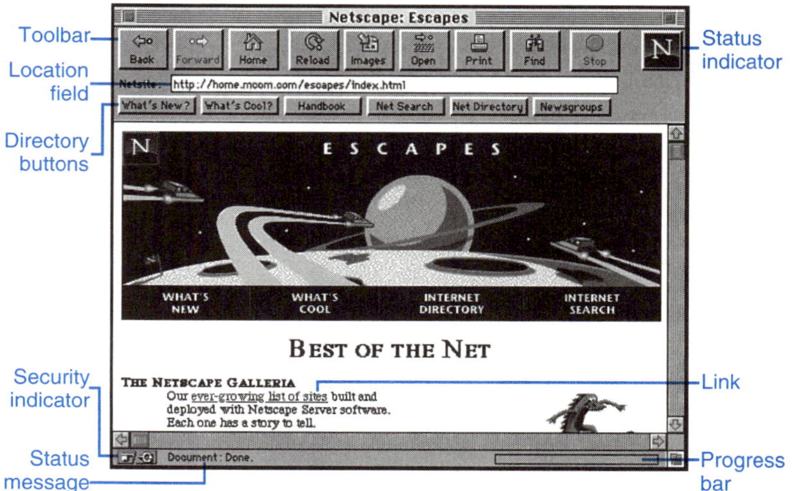

Figure 1.3 Netscape features.

- **Location field** displays the location of the Web page you are viewing. This field includes the type of connection, the name of the computer on which the site is running, and directories and any file names attached with the particular page you're viewing.
- **Status indicator** the "N" icon in the upper-right corner of the window displays a meteor shower to indicate that Netscape is downloading information. This usually occurs when you access a new page or download a file.
- **Progress bar** a red bar across the bottom of the window indicates Netscape's progress while downloading or accessing information, such as the results of a search.
- **Toolbar** icon representations of Netscape's most commonly used commands (see Lessons 2 and 3 for more explanation of what these buttons do).

- **Directory buttons** these instantly take you to preconfigured New, Cool, Searching, or other Web sites of interest.
- **Security indicator** indicates the security level of a particular page; a solid, highlighted key indicates a high level of security; a broken key indicates a low or no level of security.
- **Status message** shows messages of importance to you, such as links, document names, or status.
- **Link** indicates a clickable connection to another page on the World Wide Web. Links are represented by unique colors (usually red or blue) and can also appear underlined so that you can find them quickly. Graphics with colored borders also indicate links.

GETTING HELP ONLINE

Help for Netscape is only available online. As with other Macintosh programs, you can click any item under the Help menu. Netscape provides a lot of information on its Help menu in addition to help. For instance, you'll also see listings on security, registration, and release notes.

One of the first things you might want to look at is the Netscape Navigator—Frequently Asked Questions (FAQ).

To look at this document, open the Help menu and choose the Frequently Asked Questions option. This page has answers to many common questions (see Figure 1.4).

The best source of online help is Netscape's Handbook. You can instantly access the Handbook by clicking Netscape's Handbook button.

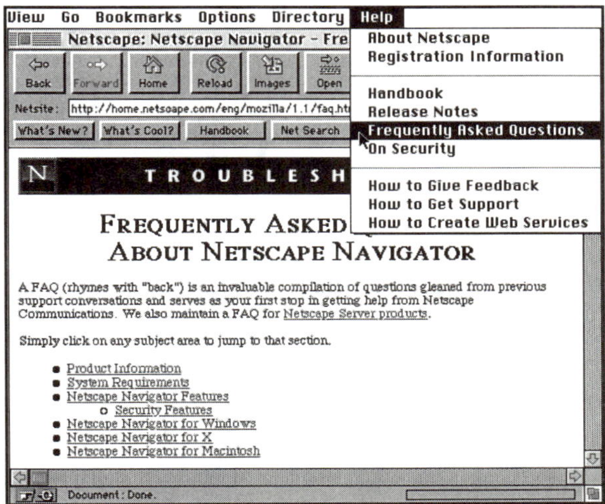

FIGURE 1.4 Netscape's Frequently Asked Questions page and how to get there.

QUITTING NETSCAPE

To quit Netscape, open the File menu and choose the Quit option (or press ⌘+Q).

In this lesson, you learned about important screen elements, how to start and quit Netscape, and where and how to get help. In the next lesson, you learn how to navigate using Netscape's toolbar.

LESSON

2 Navigating and Jumping to Your First Web Site

In this lesson, you learn about Netscape's toolbar and how to use the four navigational buttons.

What Is the Toolbar?

Netscape's toolbar is a set of buttons that you can use to quickly execute the most commonly used commands in Netscape. The toolbar is located at the top of the Netscape window directly below the title bar (see Figure 2.1).

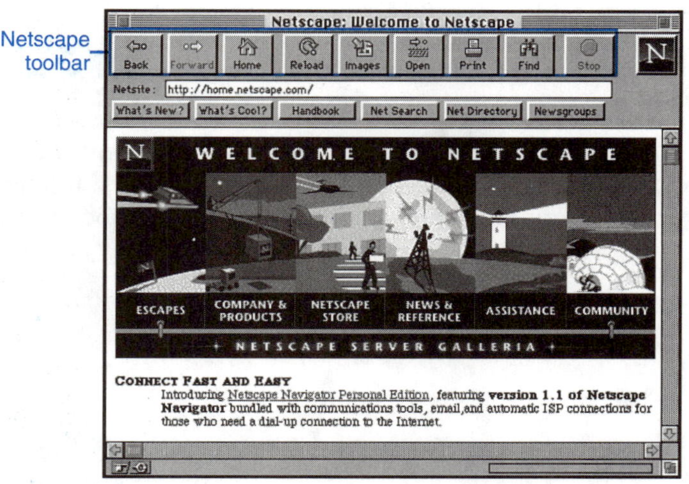

Figure 2.1 Netscape's toolbar.

There are nine Netscape toolbar buttons in all. This lesson gives an explanation of the four navigational buttons. The remaining five buttons are explained in the next lesson.

First, let's take a look at how each of the main navigational buttons in the toolbar—Home, Forward, Back, and Open—works.

USING THE OPEN BUTTON TO JUMP TO WEB SITES

The Open button is used to jump to a new *page*, sometimes referred to as a *site*, on the World Wide Web (from now on, it will be referred to simply as the Web). Just as you "open" a book to read its pages, so too must you "open" a site to see its pages.

1. Click the Open button (or press ⌘+L); the Open Location dialog box appears (see Figure 2.2).

Another Way To Get There You can also open a Web site by entering its URL in the Location field directly beneath the toolbar and pressing Return. This saves you the trouble of opening the Open Location dialog box.

FIGURE 2.2 The Open Location dialog box.

2. Type the following URL to go to the White House home page:

   http://www.whitehouse.gov/

3. Click the Open button. After waiting several seconds, the White House home page appears (see Figure 2.3).

FIGURE 2.3 The White House home page.

URL URL stands for Uniform Resource Locator. A URL allows Web browsers like Netscape to locate resources, such as Gopher and FTP sites, on the Web. Table 2.1 gives some examples of different types of URLS. Notice that all URLs begin with the type of resource, followed by **://** and the address of the computer.

TABLE 2.1 EXAMPLES OF DIFFERENT URLS

RESOURCE	SAMPLE URL
U.S. Senate Gopher	**gopher://gopher.senate.gov/**
FTP archive	**ftp://wuarchive.wustl.edu/**
White House Web page	**http://www.whitehouse.gov/**

Resource	Sample URL
FedWorld Database	**telnet://fedworld.gov/**

The White House Did Not Appear! URLs are case-sensitive, so make sure you typed it exactly as it is shown in step 2, not:

http://www.WhiteHouse.Gov

or

http://WWW.whitehouse.GOV

Also make sure that you used forward slashes (//) and not backslashes (\\) in the address.

Of course, it's also possible that this popular site is simply busy; you may have to try later.

Going Backward and Forward

The Back and Forward buttons are used primarily as navigational tools after you have viewed a series of pages. The Back button is used to take you back to the most recent page you viewed. The Forward button is used to take you forward one page.

Because you have already gone forward one page from Netscape's home page, you can click the Back button to return there. Before doing that, though, let's look at one more page.

1. The Welcome to the White House page has a map of different places you can go. Click the circle marked Executive Branch. This takes you to the page shown in Figure 2.4.
2. Next, click the Back button. You return to the White House home page.
3. Now click the Forward button. You go back to the Executive Branch page.

It might be a good idea at this point to click a couple of links from the Executive Branch page and practice using the Forward and Back buttons.

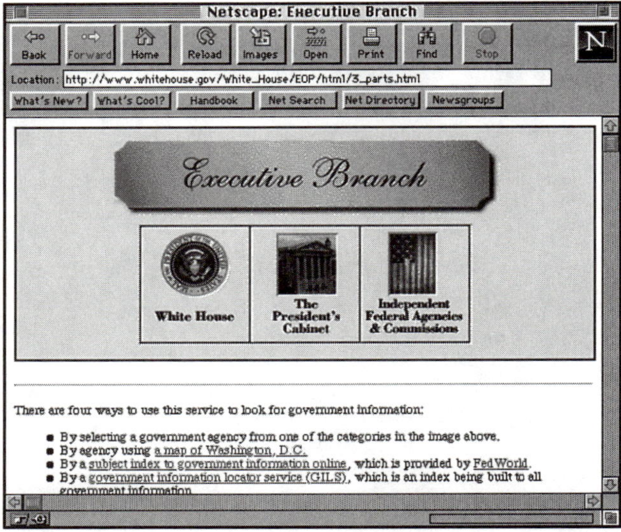

FIGURE 2.4 The Executive Branch page.

RETURNING HOME

The Home button is used to return to Netscape's home page. Simply click the Home button to return there.

Just for fun, click Open and try visiting a few of the Web sites listed on the inside covers of this book. Use this opportunity to practice using the Forward and Back buttons.

In this lesson, you learned how to use the four navigational buttons in Netscape. In the next lesson, you learn how to use the remaining toolbar buttons.

Non-Navigational Buttons on the Toolbar

In this lesson, you learn how to use the remaining buttons on Netscape's toolbar.

Netscape's Other Buttons

In Lesson 2, you learned about four buttons in Netscape's toolbar that are commonly used to navigate the Web. In this lesson, you learn about the remaining five "non-navigational" buttons: Stop, Reload, Images, Print, and Find.

Using Stop and Reload

You've probably noticed that each time you jump to a new Web page, it takes several seconds for all of the graphics and text to download so they can be displayed on your screen. Depending on how fast your modem connection is and how many graphics there are on any given page, these few seconds can easily turn into several minutes.

More Speed The faster your modem, the faster you can download information from the Web. You should be using at least a 14.4 modem, and preferably a 28.8, to use the Web effectively.

Sometimes you may not want to wait for all of the graphics on a particular page to download. For instance, if you've seen a particular page many times, you may not want or need to see the graphics again.

If this is the case, the Stop button is for you. Click the Stop button to abort the downloading of graphics so you can get right to the business of reading the text and links on a Web page.

Download Download simply means to copy a file from another computer to yours. When you jump to a new Web page, Netscape automatically downloads the text and graphic files from that page to your computer for display.

When a graphic file is downloading to your computer, you'll see a number of messages displayed in the status message area at the bottom of the Netscape window. Some common messages you'll see, and what they mean, are shown in the following table.

STATUS MESSAGE	MEANING
Transferring data	This tells you that data is being downloaded to your computer
Connect: Contacting Host:	The host computer is being contacted by your computer
Reading File	A file is being readied for download
***X*% of *X*K**	A certain percentage of a given file has been downloaded
Document: Done	The entire Web page has been successfully downloaded to your computer

Messages? What Messages? Quite often, the messages at the bottom of the screen flash by too quickly to even read. Don't worry, as long as they are flashing by, everything is okay.

The Reload button is used to reload a graphic file or files that were not successfully downloaded to your computer. This can occur either when you use the Stop button or when transmission is interrupted by your service or the host computer.

What's That Message? Sometimes, it seems like the Internet gives more busy signals than the phone company. When it does, Netscape displays a message like that shown in Figure 3.1. Don't worry about it; just try again later.

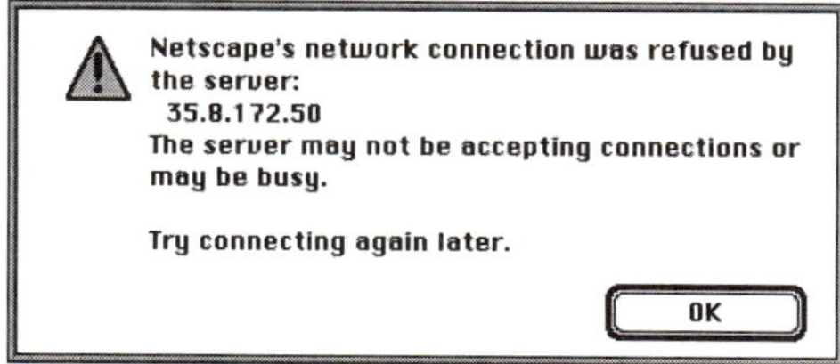

FIGURE 3.1 A busy server message.

Here's how to use the Stop and Reload buttons:

1. Click the Open button and type **http://www.cmu.edu**.
2. When the messages begin displaying in the status message area, click the Stop button. Your screen should look something like Figure 3.2.

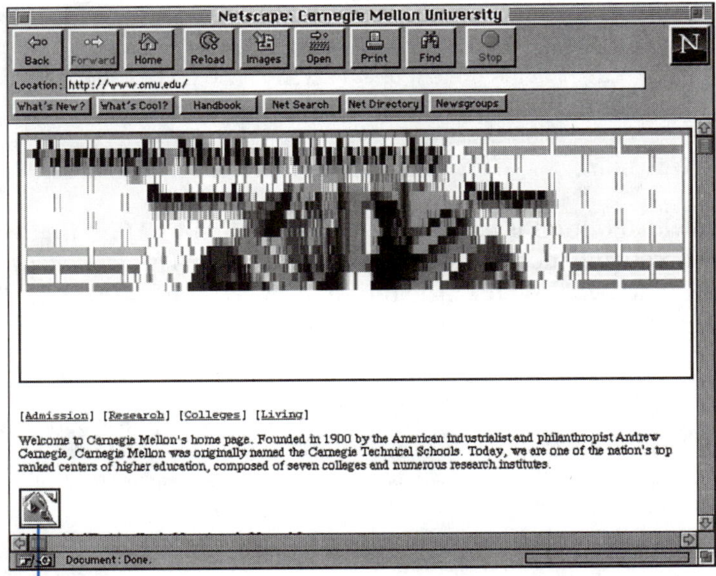

FIGURE 3.2 Using the Stop button to abort a file download.

Do I Reload Links? If you look again at Figure 3.2, you'll notice there is a bordered square with little pieces in it in the lower-left corner of the screen. This is what is often referred to as a *broken image*—in other words, an image that was not downloaded successfully. If this broken image represents a link, you can still click it without having to reload the image it represents.

3. Now click the Reload button and wait for the images to properly download. When the Web page has been fully loaded, it will look like Figure 3.3.

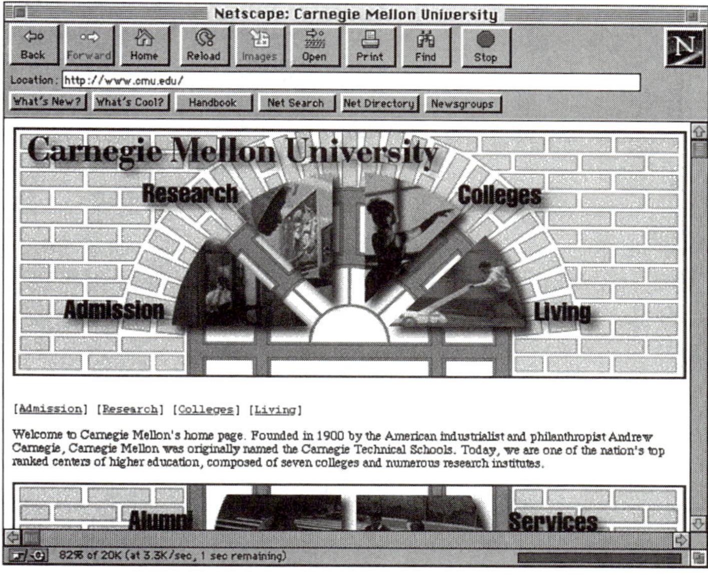

FIGURE 3.3 The Carnegie Mellon University home page.

FIND IT!

The Find button is a very useful one, especially if you have downloaded a very long Web page full of text. The Find button helps you locate text within a currently displayed Web page. Here's an example of how it works:

1. Click the Open button, type **http://www.mit.edu** in the resulting dialog box, and press Return or click Open.

   This takes you to the Massachusetts Institute of Technology home page.

2. Click the Find button to display the Find dialog box.

3. Type **fun** and click the Find button (see Figure 3.4). Netscape takes you to the first place that the letters **fun** are found. If nothing can be found, Netscape sounds a beep and returns you to the Web page.

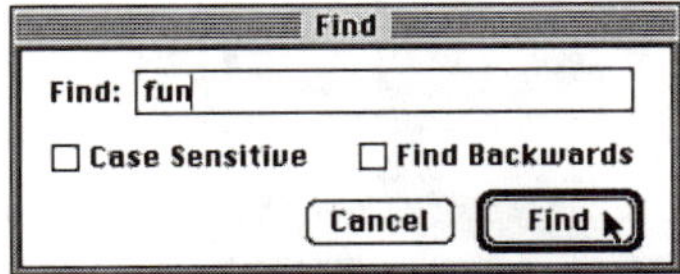

FIGURE 3.4 Searching for fun in the Find dialog box.

4. Next, scroll back up to the top of the page and click the Find button. Search for **mit people** and click Find to find. This takes you to the one instance of **mit people**.

There Aren't any MIT People! You probably didn't scroll back up to the top of the page. Netscape only looks forward (unless you select the Find Backwards check box in the Find dialog box), so if you left Netscape pointing at **fun**, it wouldn't have looked back up the page to find **MIT People**.

Every time you click the Find button, Netscape fills in the Find dialog box with the search term last used. Simply pressing Return or clicking Find finds the next instance of a term on the Web page.

You'll also notice in our example that Netscape searches for one word or several words and that Netscape makes matches regardless of letter case. If you want your search to be case-sensitive, simply select the Case Sensitive check box in the Find dialog box before clicking Find.

PRINT IT!

The Print button does just what you would expect—it prints the current page exactly as it appears on the screen. To print the MIT home page:

1. First, make sure your printer is properly selected in the Chooser Control Panel.

2. Click the Print button. In a few moments, the entire MIT home page prints out.

In this lesson, you learned how to use the remaining five toolbar buttons. In the next lesson, you learn about “links” and how to move through a Web page.

How To Move Through a Web Page Using Links

In this lesson, you learn about links and how to navigate Web pages.

What Are Links?

As you can probably already tell from the few sites you've visited, Web pages are more than just isolated locations on the World Wide Web. The vast majority of pages you'll see contain connections to other Web pages. These connections are called *links*.

Links are based on a concept from the field of hypermedia. Basically, *hypermedia* is a way of allowing a user to access different resources, such as text, sound, and graphics, in a non-linear fashion. Whereas you must start with page 1 in a book and read one page after another until you get to the last page, with hypermedia you can freely jump around through the use of links.

How To Identify Links

When using Netscape, most Web page links are easy to identify. Let's go to a Web page that has a lot of links, the WeatherNet home page (see Figure 4.1). Click the Open icon on the toolbar. In the resulting dialog box, type:

http://cirrus.sprl.umich.edu/wxnet/

As you scroll down through the first few paragraphs, notice that some of the words and phrases are underlined and displayed in a different color.

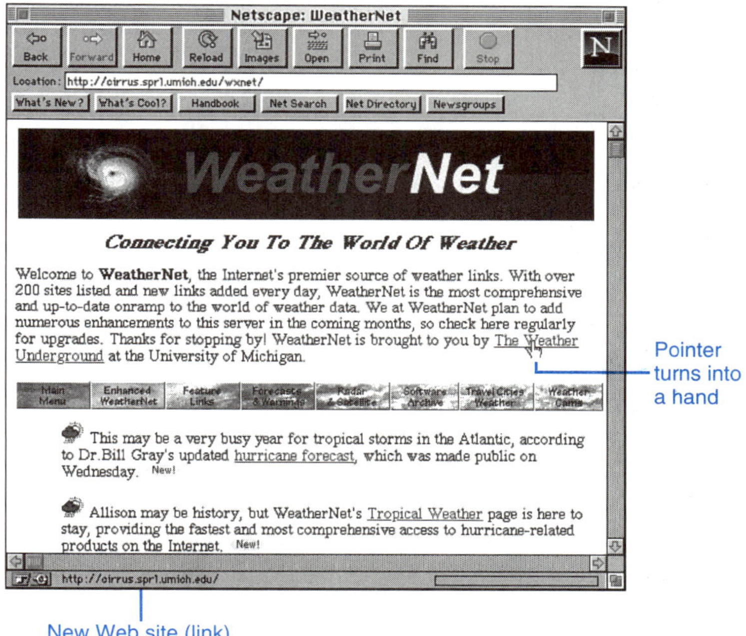

Figure 4.1 A Web link on the WeatherNet home page.

If you position the pointer on the underlined text, notice that it turns into a hand and Netscape displays the name of a new Web site in the status message line, as shown in Figure 4.1. This is a link.

Many Web page images also represent links. Images that are surrounded by a colored border always represent links. However, a lot of other images that don't have colored borders are also links. To determine if a non-bordered image is a link, just move the pointer over it. If it turns into a hand, it's a link.

Now it's time to explore and practice navigating a few links:

1. Click the link titled The Weather Underground (at the top of the WeatherNet page in the first paragraph). The Weather Underground home page appears (see Figure 4.2).

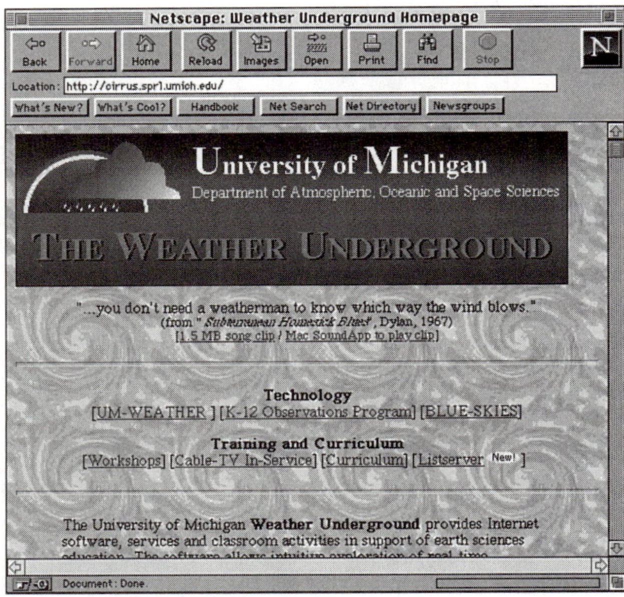

FIGURE 4.2 The Weather Underground home page.

2. Click the Back button to return to the WeatherNet home page.
3. On the graphic bar below the first paragraph, click the Feature Links button.
4. On the Feature Links page, click Lightning Photos in the second bullet (rain cloud). This takes you to the page pictured in Figure 4.3.
5. Finally, click Huge streak to the south to view the wonderful lightning image seen in Figure 4.4.

Feel free to explore additional links and look at more pictures to become more familiar with this method of navigation.

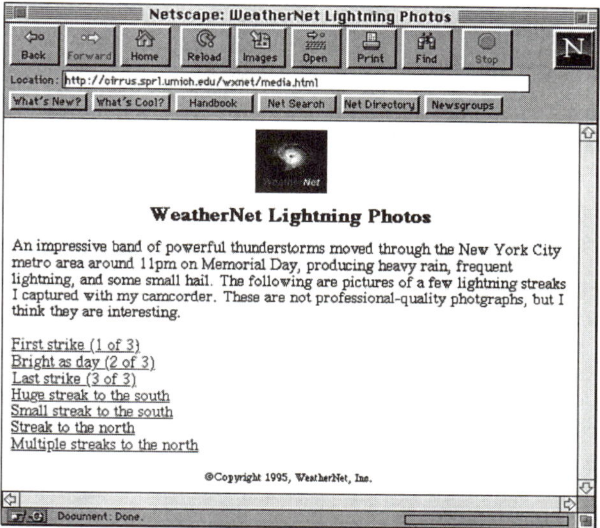

FIGURE 4.3 A choice of lightning photos.

FIGURE 4.4 The Web's version of lightning.

TRACING YOUR LINKS

To see where you've been, click the Back button several times. As you view each previous page, notice that the link you followed earlier has changed color! This is one way Netscape lets you know which Web pages you've visited. Netscape will keep these links marked in this manner for 30 days. (The amount of time Netscape keeps them can be changed, as you'll discover in Lesson 24.)

Now click the Forward button and you'll return to some of the pages you just left. You will probably notice that these pages loaded *a lot* faster than they did when you first accessed them.

That's because Netscape stores, or *caches,* each page you visit during an online session so that if you want to revisit a page, you can. However, only the pages you've visited during a single session are stored. The next time you use Netscape, these stored pages will have to be reloaded.

Cache A cache is simply a place (usually the hard drive) on a computer where information is stored. Because most computers have a lot more space available on the hard disk than they do in RAM (Random-Access Memory), many pieces of software, such as Netscape, store this information in a cache in order to save precious RAM. You'll learn more about cache later.

In this lesson, you learned how to move through a Web page and what links are. In the next lesson, you learn how to use Netscape's History feature.

Using History To See Where You've Been

LESSON 5

In this lesson, you learn how to use Netscape's History feature.

What Is the Netscape History Feature?

In Lesson 4, you learned how to use links to travel from Web page to Web page. Even with the limited exploring you've already done, you may be thinking that you could get lost very easily. All those links, pages, graphics, and Web sites—how do you know where you've been?

Fortunately, Netscape keeps track of where you've been. Just like your doctor keeps track of each one of your visits in a file of your patient history, Netscape keeps track of all your Web visits in an electronic history file. As you visit different sites on the Web, Netscape records this information for you.

Creating Your History

To see how Netscape's History feature works, you need to create some history first. You need a Web site that offers numerous links to explore. Let's start by visiting the Smithsonian Institution in Washington, D.C.

1. Click the Open toolbar button. In the Open Location dialog box, type:

   http://www.si.edu/

If this address is busy, you can try the Smithsonian's mirror site at **http://www.si.sgi.com/sgistart.htm**. This takes you to the Smithsonian home page (see Figure 5.1).

Figure 5.1 The Smithsonian home page.

Mirror Sometimes a very busy site will set up a duplicate location for its site somewhere else on the Net so that more people can have access. This duplicate site is called a *mirror*.

2. On the home page, click the What's New icon. The first link on the next page is NEW AND TEMPORARY EXHIBITIONS—click that link.
3. On the New Exhibitions page, there are a number of links. Click the one titled National Air and Space Museum to go to that page.

4. Notice that there is another link at the very top of this page—National Air and Space Museum. Click this link to get to the page shown in Figure 5.2.

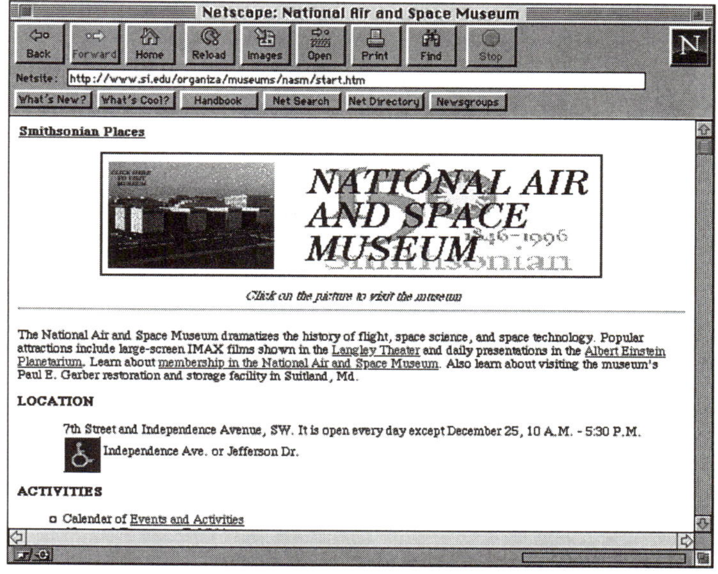

FIGURE 5.2 National Air and Space Museum home page.

By now you might be saying, "Enough already! Get on with it!" Remember, however, that you have to build a history before you can use it. Let's just click a couple more links and you'll be ready to use the History feature.

5. Scroll down to the bottom of the page and click the blue Resources icon. On the resources page, scroll down to and click the Smithsonian Photos link.

USING THE VIEW HISTORY FEATURE

Whew! You're done. It's taken a while, but the wait will be worth it. Not only will you learn how to use the History feature, but you'll have an opportunity to look at some really cool pictures.

First, let's use the History feature. Suppose you want to quickly go back to the National Air and Space Museum. To do so, simply open the Go menu and choose the National Air and Space Museum option (see Figure 5.3).

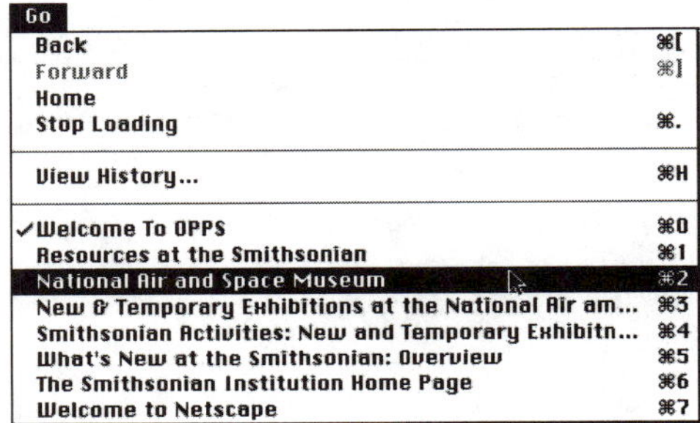

FIGURE 5.3 Using History to tell where you've been.

Use That Keyboard! You may have noticed that each page recorded in your history (under the Go menu) has a number next to it. The numbers correspond to the order in which you visited each page. You can use these keyboard combinations (⌘+2 to go to the National Air and Space Museum, for example) to instantly go to the 10 most recently visited pages.

But what if you want to go from page to page without always having to consult the Go menu or remember keyboard combinations? Is there another way? Yes, there is.

Open the Go menu again, but this time choose the View History option. The resulting window gives you a list of all the pages you've visited during a given session (see Figure 5.4).

To go to another page, simply click the item you wish to go to and then click the Go To button. Notice that Netscape places a check mark next to the page you are currently viewing. (You learn how to use the Add to Bookmarks option in the next lesson.)

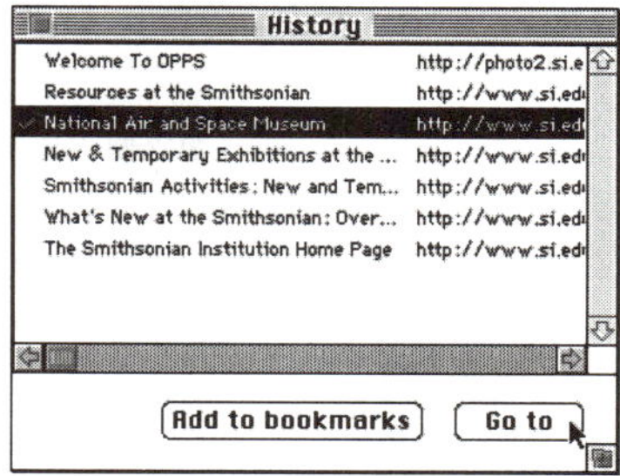

FIGURE 5.4 Netscape's History window.

A nice feature of the View History window is that you can keep it open in the background. This allows you to simply click the View History window to activate it and go to a new page at any time.

A Short History Oh, no! You've visited 15 or 20 pages and your history only shows about 10. What happened? Well, the amount of items Netscape can keep in its history depends upon how much disk space you have and how much you tell Netscape it can use. Configuring this setting to allow for a longer history is covered in detail in Lesson 24, "Configuring Netscape."

You now have two new powerful tools at your disposal that allow you to browse the Web even more efficiently. Feel free to experiment and practice—and make sure to look at some of those great pictures while you're at it!

In this lesson, you learned how to use Netscape's History feature. Unfortunately, the history of where you've been is wiped out as soon as you quit Netscape. Never fear, however. In the next lesson, you learn how to keep a permanent record of important sites you visit by using Netscape's Bookmark feature.

Creating and Using Bookmarks

In this lesson, you learn how to set bookmarks in Netscape and use them to return to previously visited Web sites.

Understanding Bookmarks

In the previous lesson, you learned that Netscape keeps a history of Web pages that you visit during a session. You also learned how to use this feature to quickly access these pages in any order to get where you want to go.

However, you also discovered that this history lasts only as long as your current Netscape session. All of the interesting and cool pages you visited are forgotten the next time you use Netscape.

Fortunately, Netscape does have a feature called a *bookmark* that allows you to keep a permanent marker of any page you want. In Netscape, bookmarks are set very much like they are in the real world.

When you're reading a book and you want to remember where you left off, you place some sort of marker in that page so that you can come right back to it the next time you read. Netscape does the same thing electronically.

When you tell Netscape, "I want to remember my place by making a bookmark," Netscape makes a note of the page's URL, name, the date you added it to your bookmark list, and the last time you visited the site so that the next time you use Netscape, you can open the Web to the right page.

Creating Bookmarks

While Netscape automatically marks Web pages in a history list, making bookmarks requires a little effort on your part. Happily for you, doing so is a fairly simple, straightforward procedure. To practice making bookmarks, let's visit a few new sites and make a bookmark for each one.

1. Using the method you prefer, go to **http://www.apple.com/**. This takes you to Apple's home page (see Figure 6.1).

Figure 6.1 Apple's home page.

2. Open the Bookmarks menu and choose the Add Bookmark option (or press ⌘+D). This places the Apple home page into your bookmark list.
3. Repeat steps 1 and 2 for the following Web sites:

   http://espnet.sportszone.com/ (ESPNet SportsZone)

http://www.census.gov/ (U.S. Census Bureau)

http://www.novell.com/ (Novell, Inc.)

Too Many Bookmarks It will be tempting to begin making bookmarks every time you see a page that might be of interest. Resist this urge, however, because making too many bookmarks defeats the purpose of making them (imagine trying to find one bookmark among 200!). Make sure that you'll want to visit a page often before you create a bookmark for it.

4. To view your new bookmark list, open the Bookmarks menu and choose the View Bookmarks option (or press ⌘+B).

Your bookmark list should now look like the one shown in Figure 6.2.

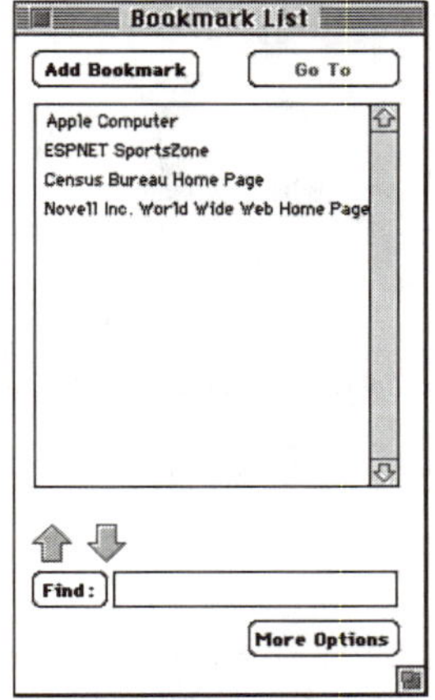

FIGURE 6.2 Bookmark List with four Web sites added.

My Window's Too Big If your Bookmark List window shows more options than the one pictured in Figure 6.2, don't worry. Just click the Fewer Options button and your window will look like Figure 6.2. You'll learn about some of the other options in the Bookmark List window in Lessons 7 and 8.

If you look at your history list by choosing the View History option from the Go menu, you'll notice that the same four items appear. However, just to confirm the difference between history and bookmarks:

1. Exit Netscape by opening the File menu and choosing the Quit option (or press ⌘+Q).
2. Double-click the Netscape icon to restart Netscape.
3. After you've restarted Netscape, open the Go menu. The four bookmarks you just created are not there.
4. Now, open the Bookmarks menu and you'll see that the pages you just added are still on your list (see Figure 6.3).

FIGURE 6.3 List of bookmarks containing the previous four saved pages.

To use your new bookmarks, simply open the Bookmarks menu and choose the item you would like to go to. For example, to return to the ESPNet SportsZone, simply choose the ESPNet SportsZone item in the Bookmarks menu and you will instantly go to its Web page.

In this lesson, you learned how to set and use bookmarks. In the next lesson, you learn how to edit and delete bookmarks.

EDITING AND DELETING BOOKMARKS

In this lesson, you learn how to edit and delete bookmarks from your bookmark list.

EDITING BOOKMARKS

In the previous lesson, you learned how to add Web pages to your bookmark list. You discovered that this is an excellent way to keep track of pages you like, as well as a quick way to return to them anytime you like. Bookmark lists are a permanent and easy way to keep track of your travels on the Web.

As you'll discover in this lesson and the next, bookmarks offer other features that can make them even more useful to you. In this lesson, you learn how to delete and edit bookmarks.

You may have noticed in the last lesson that Netscape simply uses the Web page title to describe the bookmark. Many times this information is enough. However, if you have numerous bookmarks, you may want to add to or rename a bookmark title to better suit your needs.

To help you do this, Netscape allows you to edit your bookmarks. This feature lets you customize each bookmark to maximize its usefulness to you. Let's go to another page on the Web and use it to learn how the bookmark editing feature of Netscape works.

1. Using the method you prefer, go to **http://www.disney.com/**. This takes you to the Disney home page, which is used to showcase Disney's movies (see Figure 7.1).

Figure 7.1 Buena Vista MoviePlex—The Disney home page.

2. Open the Bookmarks menu and choose Add Bookmark (or press ⌘+D) to add this page to your bookmark list.
3. After the bookmark has been added, open the Bookmarks menu and choose the View Bookmarks option (or press ⌘+B).

   The Bookmark List window appears. If the editing portion of the window is not displayed (the Name, Location, and Description fields), simply click the More Options button and the editing options will appear.
4. In the scrollable field containing the bookmarks, click Buena Vista MoviePlex. Notice that all of the information about the bookmark, such as its name and location, is instantly displayed (see Figure 7.2).

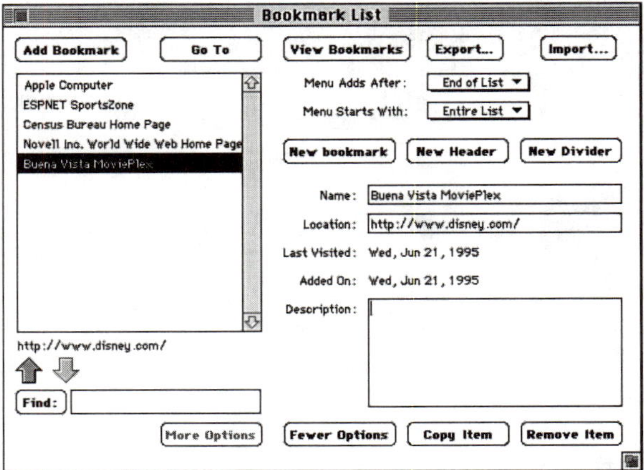

FIGURE 7.2 Buena Vista MoviePlex bookmark information.

You are now ready to edit the bookmark's name and give it a description:

1. Click in the **Name** field and replace **Buena Vista MoviePlex** by pressing the Backspace key and typing **Disney Home Page**.

2. Next, click in the **Description** field and type in a short description of this page. Your description can be up to 255 characters in length.

Your new bookmark should look something like Figure 7.3.

Your bookmark is automatically saved when you return to Netscape. Simply click the Bookmark List window's Close box to return to Netscape.

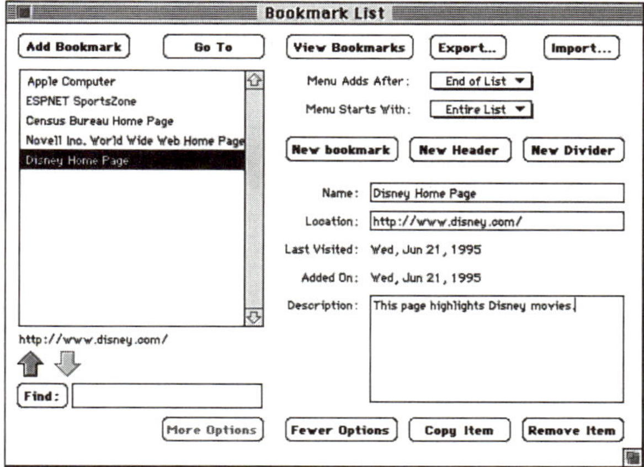

FIGURE 7.3 An edited bookmark.

DELETING BOOKMARKS

The World Wide Web is likely to be one of the fastest growing and most constantly changing places you'll ever encounter. In the beginning of 1995, it was estimated that there were roughly (and I mean *very* roughly) 1 million pages on the Web.

An exact count is virtually impossible because new pages are added daily, and old pages seem to change and disappear almost as quickly. As a result, you will find yourself adding Web pages to your bookmark list on a regular basis.

You'll also discover that you will want to delete the bookmarks for Web pages as they become outdated or simply disappear. Fortunately, deleting a Web page bookmark with Netscape is as easy as clicking a button. To practice, you will now delete the Disney bookmark. To do so:

1. Open the Bookmarks menu and choose the View Bookmarks option. The Bookmark List window appears.
2. In the scrollable field containing the bookmarks, click the Disney Home Page.
3. Click the Remove Item button.

The bookmark has now been removed.

It's Gone, But It's Not The Disney Home Page bookmark no longer shows up in the window, but its information in the Name and Description fields has remained—what's wrong? Nothing, really. You must close the Bookmark List window by clicking the Close box for all of the information to disappear. If you exit the Bookmark List window and then reopen it, you will see that this remaining information has disappeared.

In this lesson, you learned how to edit and delete bookmarks. However, even though you can now somewhat manage these bookmarks, you still haven't learned how to organize them. What happens when you have 45 bookmarks? How can you find one quickly and efficiently? To find out, turn to the next lesson.

Organizing Your Bookmarks

LESSON 8

In this lesson, you learn how to organize your random list of bookmarks.

Creating Submenus

If you're an active Web browser, it doesn't take long before your bookmark list has dozens (if not hundreds) of bookmarks. Searching through a list this big can be unwieldy, to say the least. Fortunately, Netscape has provided an easy way to organize your bookmarks so that you can use them quickly and efficiently.

Here's a typical bookmark list that has not yet been organized (see Figure 8.1).

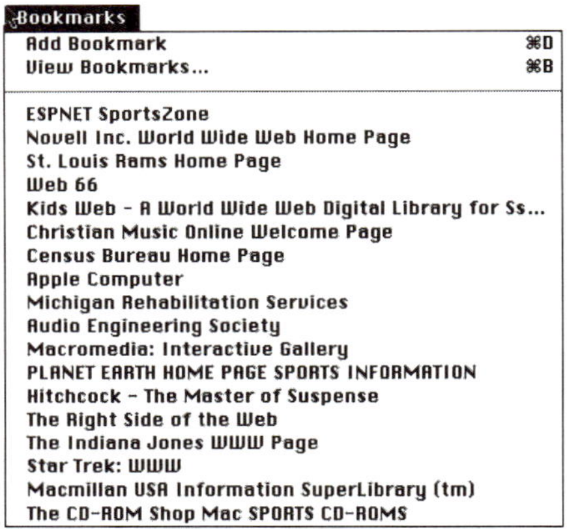

Bookmarks

Add Bookmark ⌘D
View Bookmarks... ⌘B

ESPNET SportsZone
Novell Inc. World Wide Web Home Page
St. Louis Rams Home Page
Web 66
Kids Web - A World Wide Web Digital Library for Ss...
Christian Music Online Welcome Page
Census Bureau Home Page
Apple Computer
Michigan Rehabilitation Services
Audio Engineering Society
Macromedia: Interactive Gallery
PLANET EARTH HOME PAGE SPORTS INFORMATION
Hitchcock - The Master of Suspense
The Right Side of the Web
The Indiana Jones WWW Page
Star Trek: WWW
Macmillan USA Information SuperLibrary (tm)
The CD-ROM Shop Mac SPORTS CD-ROMS

Figure 8.1 Unorganized bookmark list.

As you can see, this is just a randomly organized list of bookmarks that might be created as you browse the Web. As you can also see, many of these Web pages could very easily be organized by category—and that's exactly what you're going to do in this lesson.

First, you're going to add a few of the pages listed in Figure 8.1. Go to each one of the pages listed below and add them to your bookmark list, as you learned in Lesson 6.

> **http://www.nando.net/football/1994/nfl/fbhome/ram.html**
>
> **http://www.nosc.mil/planet_earth/sports.html**
>
> **http://www.interlog.com/~pjm/cdshop/mac/cat42.html**

Your bookmark list should now include the original four bookmarks you added in Lesson 6 plus these three new ones. You are now ready to begin organizing your bookmarks:

1. Open the Bookmarks menu and choose the View Bookmarks option (or press ⌘+B).
2. With the Bookmark List window open displaying the editing options, click the New Header button. The words **New Header** appear in the Name field.
3. Replace the words **New Header** in the Name field by typing **Sports**.

The Name Didn't Change Even though you changed the name, you'll notice that in the Bookmark List window it's still called **New Header**. Don't worry; simply click the bookmark still titled New Header in the scrollable field and it will instantly be renamed **Sports**.

4. Next, let's assume that because sports are more important than anything else in the world, you want your Sports header to be the first item in your bookmark list. Click Sports to select it and click the up arrow located above the Find button. Sports moves up one spot to the top of the list (see Figure 8.2).

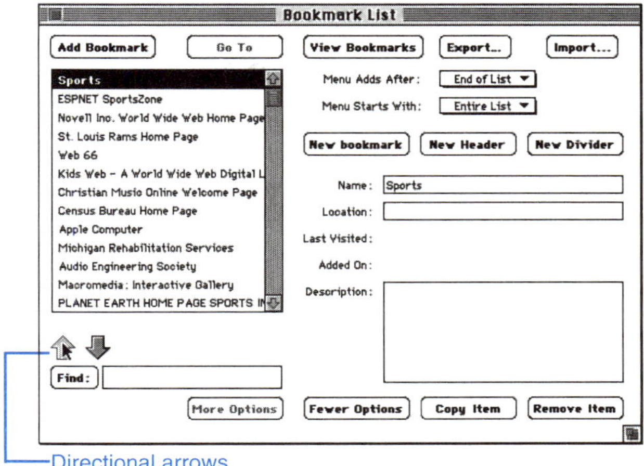

FIGURE 8.2 Moving a bookmark to the top of the list.

Now you are ready to begin organizing your bookmarks under one heading. Although you'll only be creating one heading containing four subitems in this lesson, you can create as many headings and put as many items under each heading as you'd like.

To put bookmarks under headings:

1. Click the item you want to move under the heading. (For this example, pick PLANET EARTH HOME PAGE SPORTS INFORMATION.)
2. Repeatedly click the up arrow (that you used to move the Sports heading to the top) until the **PLANET EARTH HOME PAGE SPORTS INFORMATION** item is indented under the Sports heading (see Figure 8.3).

When an Item Doesn't Indent You click the up arrow and the correct item moves under the heading, but doesn't indent? No problem; click the up arrow one more time and it will. When an item is not indented under a header, that indicates that it is simply another item that appears after the header. The indentation indicates that it is in the header's group.

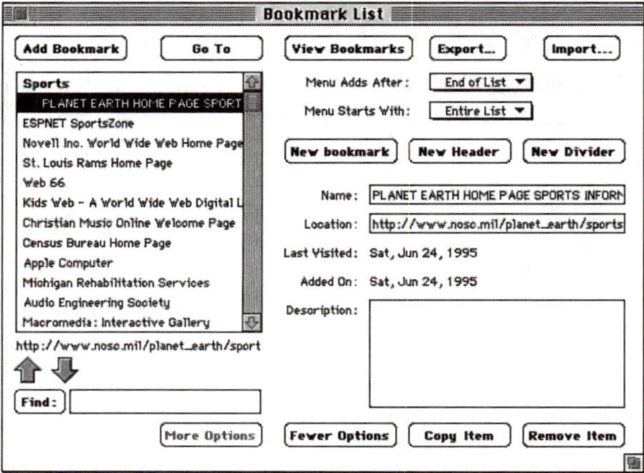

FIGURE 8.3 A subitem is added under a header.

You can now repeat steps 1 and 2 above for the rest of the sports-related Web sites you have in your bookmark list. If an item is ever above the header you want to include it under, you'll have to use the down arrow after you've highlighted it, but the process is the same. When you're done, your Sports head and subitems should look similar to Figure 8.4.

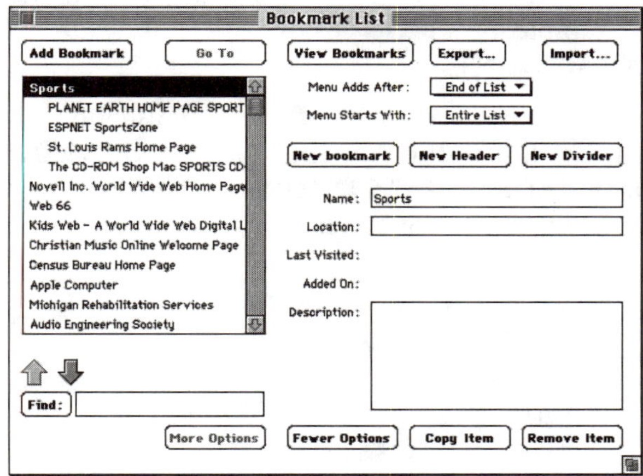

FIGURE 8.4 The Sports header with subitems.

Can't See Them All? The scrollable field that displays your bookmarks in the Bookmark List window is rather small; it only allows you to see a limited number of bookmarks at a time. This can make organizing difficult. Here's a shortcut: double-click a header. Notice that all of the subitems disappear and the header is underlined. To view the subitems again, simply double-click the header. Please note, however, that you can't add subitems to a header while it's underlined.

It's time to close the Bookmark List window and look at your handiwork. Open the Bookmarks menu. Notice that there is a new item with an arrow next to it titled **Sports.** Choose Sports (by clicking it and holding down your mouse button) and you'll see the four subitems that you added (see Figure 8.5).

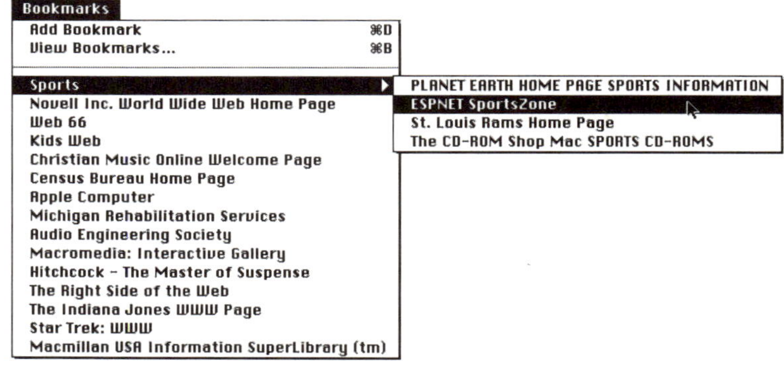

FIGURE 8.5 The Sports heading and subitems.

In this lesson, you learned how to organize a random list of bookmarks into categories for quicker access. In the next lesson, you learn how to find Web pages using keyword searches.

Searching for Web Sites by Keywords

In this lesson, you learn how to search for Web sites by keywords using the Lycos and InfoSeek search engines.

What Is a Search Engine?

With more than a million Web sites in existence and new ones popping up every day, you may have begun to wonder how anyone keeps track of them. It must be just like finding the proverbial needle in a haystack, right? Well, it is. But if you think about it, finding a needle in a haystack isn't very difficult if you have a good metal detector.

Fortunately, the Web has plenty of good "Web detectors" designed to help you find that "needle." These detectors, which are designed to find information on the Web, are called *search engines*.

Search Engine A search engine is just what it sounds like—an engine that searches. Engines are generally associated with doing work and bearing the load. Thus, an engine that searches does all of the locating "work" for you.

Access to several search engines is built into Netscape. This lesson shows you how to use two of them, InfoSeek and Lycos. Because most search engines work roughly the same, learning how to use these two will give you a good start.

To use either InfoSeek or Lycos, click the Net Search directory button and proceed to the next sections. You should start from a page that looks like the one shown in Figure 9.1.

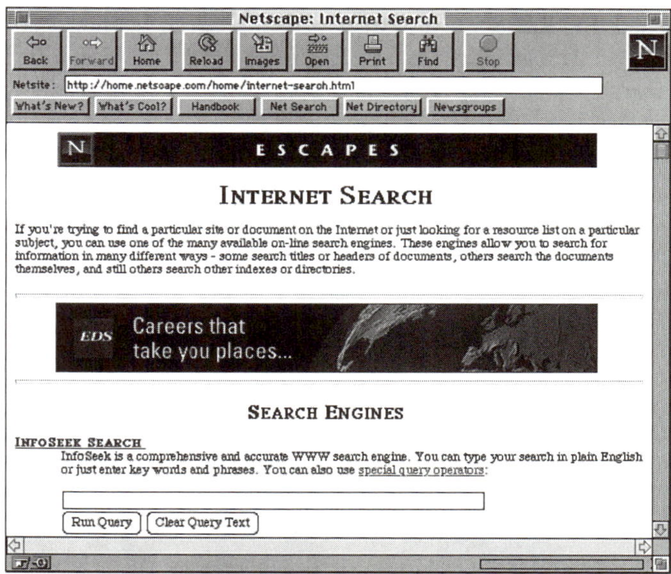

FIGURE 9.1 The Netscape Net Search page.

USING INFOSEEK

InfoSeek is both convenient and easy to use. It is convenient because it is available directly on the Net Search page and because it reliably returns useful results to your search. It is easy to use because it's practically an instant process—enter a phrase, click a button, and you're off!

1. On the Net Search page pictured in Figure 9.1, notice that the first Search Engine listed is **InfoSeek**.

2. Enter the search term you want to find (this can contain one or several words) in the InfoSeek Search field pictured

in Figure 9.1. For this example, let's look for **Indiana Jones**. Remember, you can also type **indiana jones** to get the same results because this search engine isn't case-sensitive.

3. Click the Run Query button and the search begins. Sit back and wait for InfoSeek to find *hits* that match your search.

Hit A hit is another name for result. If your search for Indiana Jones results in a Web page containing 10 links, you have 10 hits.

When InfoSeek is done, a new Web page like the one shown in Figure 9.2 is displayed. Click a hit, such as The Indiana Jones WWW Page, to see where it leads. It's really that easy.

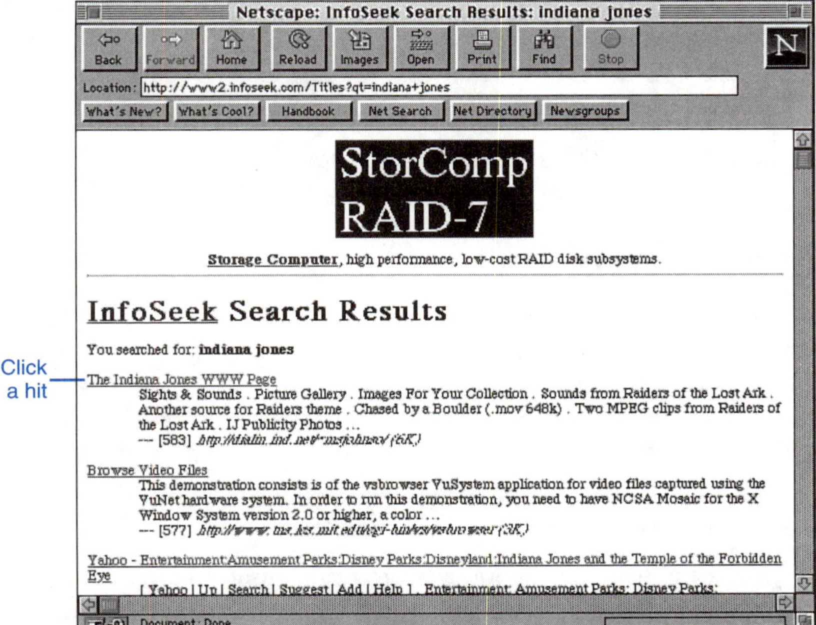

FIGURE 9.2 Results for the search Indiana Jones.

There's Not Enough! InfoSeek does have its limitations. The free version provided for you on the Net Search page only returns the first 10 hits it finds. To get more results, you'll either have to become a registered user (go to **http://www.infoseek.com:80/Home** to find out how) or use a more powerful search engine, such as Lycos.

SEARCHING WITH LYCOS

The *Lycos* search engine, run by Carnegie Mellon University, is one of the most widely used Internet search engines, and therefore, also one of the busiest. Lycos is actually two search engines in one. Lycos can search a large database comprised of almost 4.25 million Web pages (at the time of this writing), or a smaller one comprised of over 750,000 Web pages.

The standard trade-offs are there: the larger database gives you more complete results, but takes longer and may be harder to access; the smaller one gives you fewer results, but is generally faster and more accessible. You decide which database to use depending upon your own needs.

In addition to Web pages, the large Lycos database also contains information on Gopher and FTP sites (see Lessons 13 and 14 for information on using Gopher and FTP sites).

In this lesson, you will perform a search on the keywords star trek. To use Lycos from the main Net Search page:

1. Scroll down and click the link The Lycos Home Page: Hunting WWW Information (located directly below InfoSeek). This takes you to the Lycos home page (see Figure 9.3).
2. To use the big search database from the Lycos home page, select the big Lycos catalog link (to use the small database, select the link small Lycos catalog). This takes you to the Lycos search Web page shown in Figure 9.4.

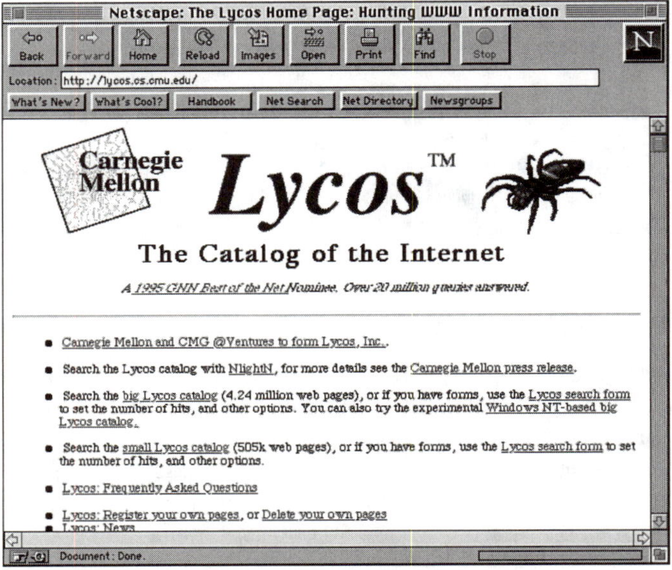

FIGURE 9.3 The Lycos home page.

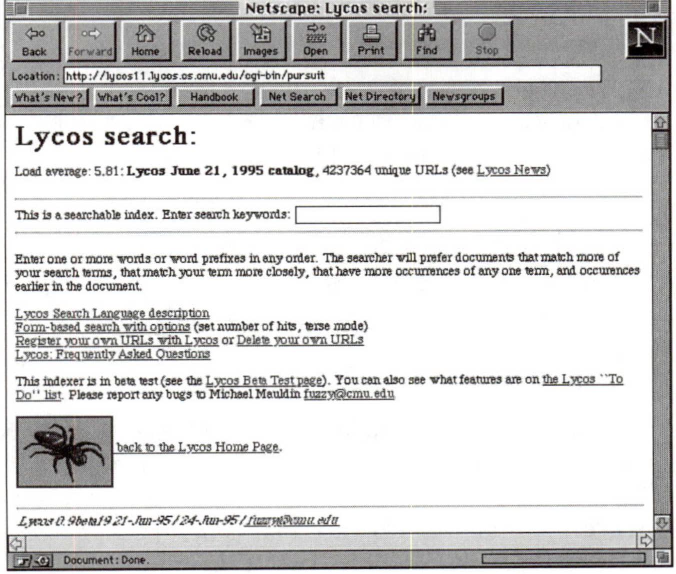

FIGURE 9.4 The big Lycos catalog search page.

Lycos Is Too Busy! Lycos is a very busy search engine. However, when it is busy, Lycos points you to alternate search pages that have been set up. When you get a Lycos Busy message, new links appear at the top of the page; these are the alternate Lycos search engines.

3. In the keywords search field, type **star trek** and press Return. After a few moments, the results of the keywords search are displayed (see Figure 9.5). You must scroll down the page a little to view the descriptive list of hits.

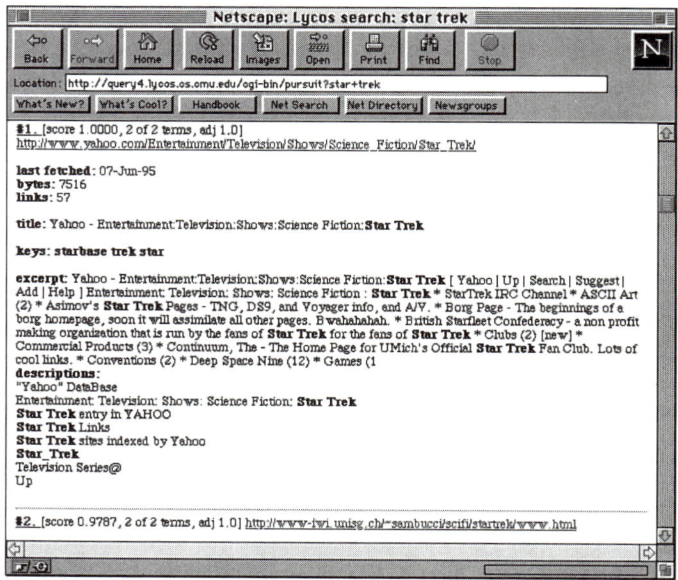

FIGURE 9.5 Results of the keywords search for star trek.

On a search for **star trek**, Lycos returned over 15,000 hits! This is because Lycos searches for instances of star, trek, and star trek. Also notice that Lycos only displays 10 hits at a time. After scrolling through the first 10, you can click the Next 10 link at the bottom of the page to see more. Sometimes you get more information than you want, but it's a safe bet that the information you are looking for is included in this list.

But if you want to conduct a more precise search, can you? Yes, you can. If you go back to the big Lycos catalog search page, you'll see that there are a number of links below the Keyword Search field.

One of these is the **Form-based search with options** link. To conduct a narrower search:

1. Click the Form-based search with options link. A new page appears that allows you to determine how many hits you want Lycos to find.
2. If, for instance, you only want 25 hits, type **25** in the Max-hits field.
3. If you want to match only **star trek**, type **2** in the Min-terms field and **star trek** in the Query field.
4. Finally, click the Start Search button. Even though Lycos still returns over 15,000 hits, only those items that meet the search criteria are displayed (see Figure 9.6).

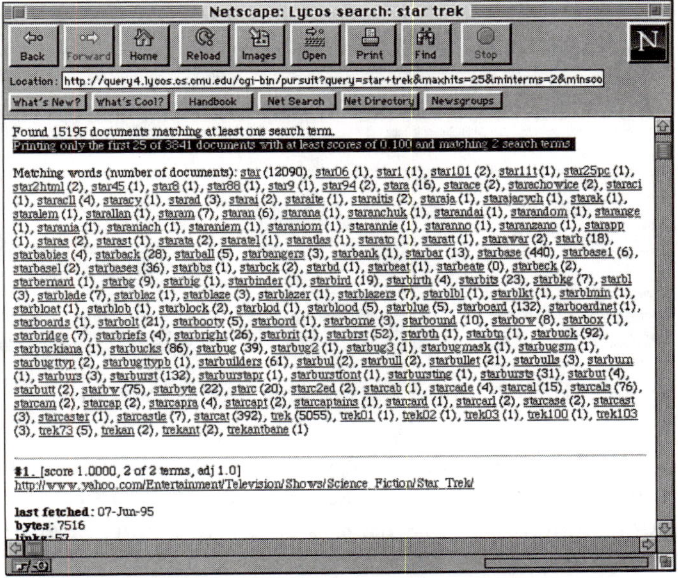

FIGURE 9.6 A narrowed search using Lycos.

In this lesson, you learned how to search for Web pages by keywords. Keyword searches, however, aren't the only way to locate Web pages. In the next lesson, you learn how to search for Web pages by category.

Lesson 10 Searching for Web Sites by Category

In this lesson, you learn how to search for Web sites by category using Yahoo and The Virtual Tourist.

Locating Web Sites by Category

In Lesson 9, you learned how to use some of the available Web search engines to locate Web pages based on keyword searches. But searching by keywords is not the only way to locate Web pages. Although effective, many people also choose to search by category. To search by category, you can use two different search engines. You can use Yahoo to search by general category and The Virtual Tourist to search by geographical category.

Searching with Yahoo

The Yahoo directory was started by David Filo and Jerry Yang when they were graduate students at Stanford University. It now contains more than 44,000 Web page listings in its database. Although these listings are only a fraction of those found on Lycos, they are still considered more accessible because they are organized by category.

To get to the Yahoo server, simply click the Net Directory button located next to the **Net Search** button you used in the last lesson. Although Yahoo does have a keyword search engine, it is primarily used for category searches. Yahoo is organized into 14 different categories.

Obviously, if you're going to perform a search by category, you need to know which category your search belongs to. In order to compare a Yahoo search to a Lycos search, let's once again look for Star Trek Web pages. From the Yahoo server page:

1. Because Star Trek is likely to be found under Entertainment, click that link.
2. You will now see a listing of each entertainment-related category Yahoo has in its database. At this point, you have two choices—**Movies and Films** or **Television**. For this example, click Television.
3. Scroll down until you see the Shows link and click it.
4. Because Star Trek was a science fiction show, click the Science Fiction link.
5. If you scroll down, you will see a Star Trek link. Click this link to see all of the listings under Star Trek (see Figure 10.1).

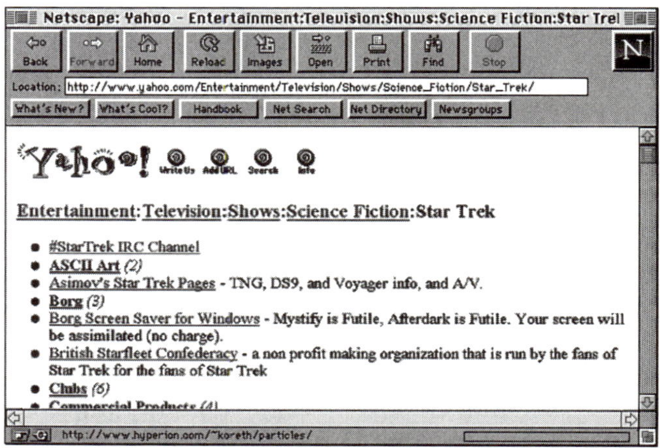

FIGURE 10.1 Yahoo's listing of Star Trek pages.

Even though it may appear that Yahoo requires more steps to get somewhere than Lycos, it really doesn't. Once you have found Star Trek, you have a listing of only those pages you want to see. If you remember, with Lycos, you had to view hits 10 at a time and wade through thousands of sites before possibly finding the one you wanted.

Keep in mind that you do need to have some idea of how the subject you're searching for is categorized. For example, if you were looking for information on computer training manuals, would you look under **Computers**, **Education**, or **Reference**? As you become more familiar with category searching, these answers become easier.

Which Category Is Right? When searching for a complicated category, such as computer training manuals, try using the biggest category first. In this case, there is probably more information on computers than there is on training (**Education**) or manuals (**Reference**). Therefore, it would be best to try searching under the **Computer** category first.

USING THE VIRTUAL TOURIST

Another popular category that many people use to search the Web is geography. Many times, people want information that may be specific or restricted to a certain geographical region. The Virtual Tourist allows you to do just that. To get there:

1. Click the Net Directory button.
2. Scroll down until you see The Virtual Tourist and click that link. This takes you to The Virtual Tourist home page (see Figure 10.2). You might note that there is another geographical search engine above the Virtual Tourist called World-Wide Web Servers. This is also an excellent site, but it can often be busy for hours at a time.

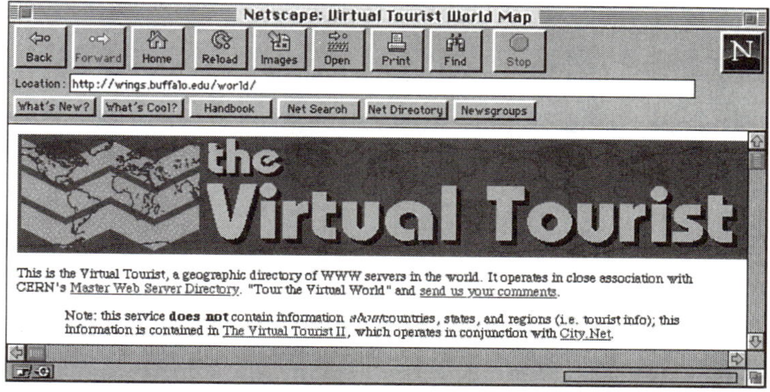

FIGURE 10.2 The Virtual Tourist home page.

But I Am a Tourist! You may have noticed that the Virtual Tourist home page says that it contains no typical "tourist" information (information about countries, states, and regions). To search for this information, click the link The Virtual Tourist II at the top of the home page.

Using the Virtual Tourist is very easy. Suppose you want to find out what's new in Japan:

1. From the Virtual Tourist home page pictured in Figure 10.2, scroll down until you see the picture of a world map.
2. Click the region marked Asia. This takes you to the Asia page.
3. Scroll down until you see the map containing Japan and click Japan.
4. Next you will see an enlarged map of Japan, with many areas highlighted. You can now go to any region in Japan you like. Because Hiroshima is a well-known city, click it. This takes you to a page similar to that shown in Figure 10.3.

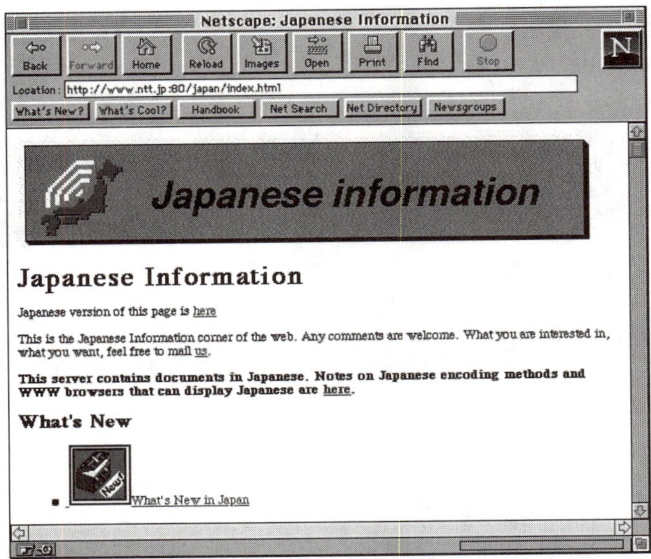

FIGURE 10.3 Web page containing information on Japan.

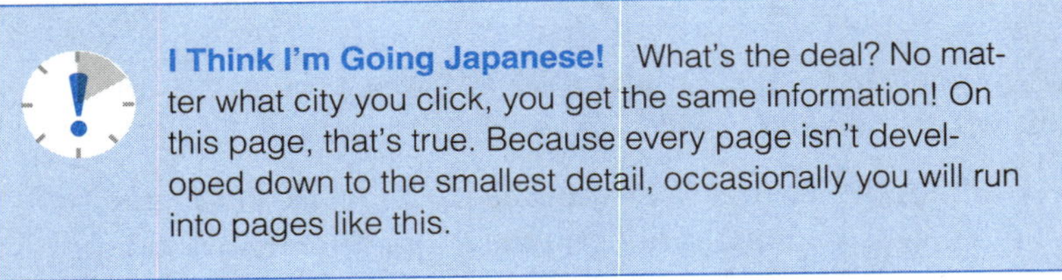

I Think I'm Going Japanese! What's the deal? No matter what city you click, you get the same information! On this page, that's true. Because every page isn't developed down to the smallest detail, occasionally you will run into pages like this.

5. You can now click the What's New in Japan link to get the latest scoop on what's what and who's who in Japan.

As you might imagine, information available via different types of searches conducted on different servers can be similar. Although there probably will be many differences in the amount and type of information available depending on how you search, the biggest difference is in how you get to where you're going.

In this lesson, you learned how to search by different categories by using Yahoo and the Virtual Tourist. In the next lesson, you learn how to search for people on the Internet.

Searching for People on the Net

In this lesson, you learn how to search for people on the Internet using the Four11 service.

Where Are the Yellow Pages?

Imagine if someone tried to collect the phone numbers of every person in the world. In our mobile society, such a task would be next to impossible. Now imagine trying to collect all of the e-mail addresses of everyone in the world. Because we can add technology and instant access of information to the equation, such a task becomes a little more doable.

However, finding someone's e-mail address is still a process that is far from perfect. With some know-how, a little luck, and some perseverance, you *can* have success.

There are several avenues you can use to search for users on the Internet. Some are difficult to use, some are not very reliable. Probably the easiest to use is the Four11 service. Not only can you find people on the Net with it, but you can also register yourself so that others can find you.

Getting Yourself on Four11

A very useful service for finding e-mail addresses on the Internet is called the Four11 Directory Service. Using Four11 involves two steps: registering yourself so that others can find your address and then using it to find others' addresses. First, you're going to get your own e-mail address on Four11's directory. To do so:

1. Open the Directory menu and choose the Internet White Pages option. This takes you to the People and Places page (Figure 11.1).

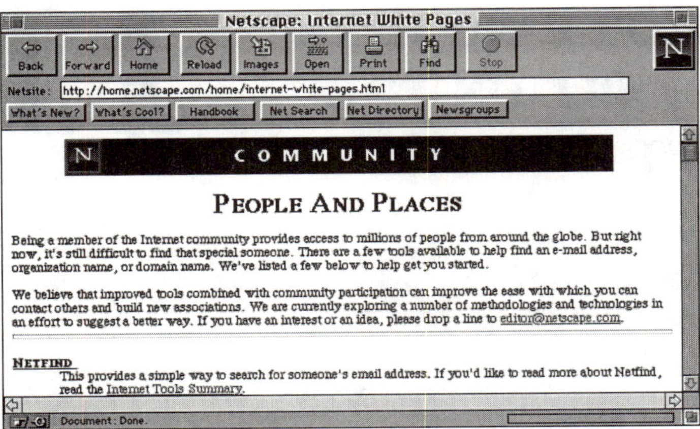

FIGURE 11.1 People and Places page.

2. Scroll down until you see the Four11 service and click the link. This takes you to the screen shown in Figure 11.2.

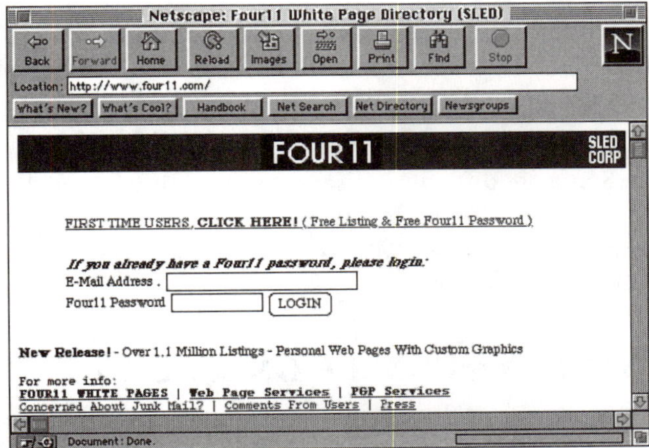

FIGURE 11.2 The Four11 directory service.

3. Because you have probably never used the Four11 service, click the First Time Users link to register your e-mail address.

4. You will be asked for your name, address, and e-mail address, among other things. The fields pictured in Figure 11.3 *must* be filled in.

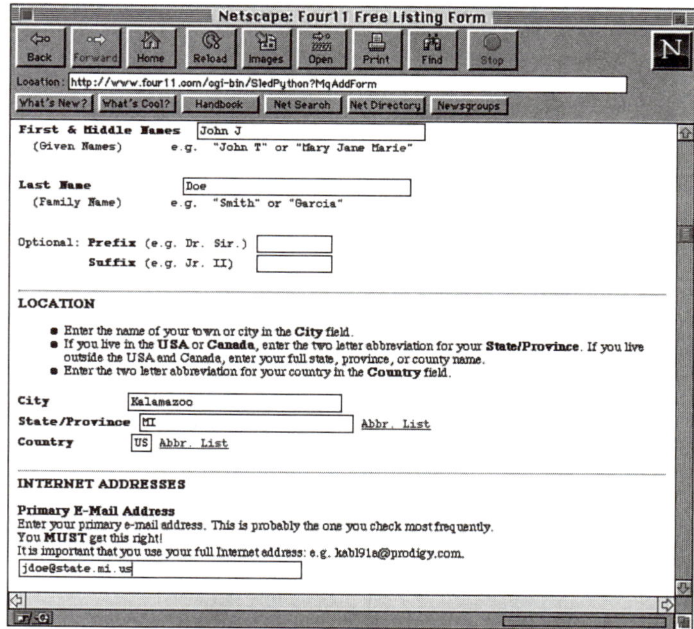

FIGURE 11.3 Information to register with Four11.

As you scroll down the page, you can fill in the other optional areas if you like (see Table 11.1 for a description of each field).

TABLE 11.1 REGISTERING WITH FOUR11

FIELD	INFORMATION	REQUIRED
First & Middle Names	Your first and middle name or middle initial	Yes
Last Name	Your last name	Yes
Prefix	Titles such as Dr.	No

continues

TABLE 11.1 CONTINUED

FIELD	INFORMATION	REQUIRED
Suffix	Titles such as Jr. or Sr.	No
City	Your city of residence	Yes
State/Province	Your state (U.S.) or Province (Canada) of residence	Yes
Country	Your country of residence	Yes
Primary E-Mail Address	Your e-mail address	Yes
Additional E-Mail Address	If you have any more addresses you'd like to register	No
Old E-Mail Address	If you have a previous address registered with Four11	No
Personal URL	If you have your own Web page, enter it here	No
Group Connections	These three categories allow you to provide personal information about who you are	No

Spam! Spam is a term used on the Internet to refer to electronic junk mail. Many people are afraid to register themselves with any service for fear of receiving this type of mail. Four11 goes to great lengths to prevent this, although the possibility of someone sending you Spam from your Four11 listing does exist.

5. Scroll down to the bottom of the page and click the Submit Form button. Your password will be e-mailed to you.

You must wait a maximum of 24 hours for your new listing to be registered with Four11. Your password generally is sent to you within a half-hour of registering (but it can take longer).

SEARCHING FOR USERS WITH FOUR11

You can now search for other people on the Internet using Four11. To do so:

1. Open the Directory menu and choose the Internet White Pages option.
2. Scroll down until you see the Four11 service and click the link.
3. Instead of clicking **First Time Users**, simply type in the ***e-mail address*** and ***password*** Four11 e-mailed to you and click the LOGIN button.
4. You will be shown several options on the next page. Click the Search Directory link.
5. On the Search page, you will be able to look under a number of options. Enter as much information as you can about the person you are looking for. Figure 11.4 is an example of information you might provide for your search. Click the Search button to begin.

I Couldn't Find You There are a couple of things to watch out for when conducting a search. First, if you provide State/Province information, you must also provide the Country code. Second, you cannot use the Surf, All Wildcards, Sleeper Search, or Domain options unless you register as a paying user of Four11 (which you can do by choosing UPGRADE membership option from the screen in Step 2).

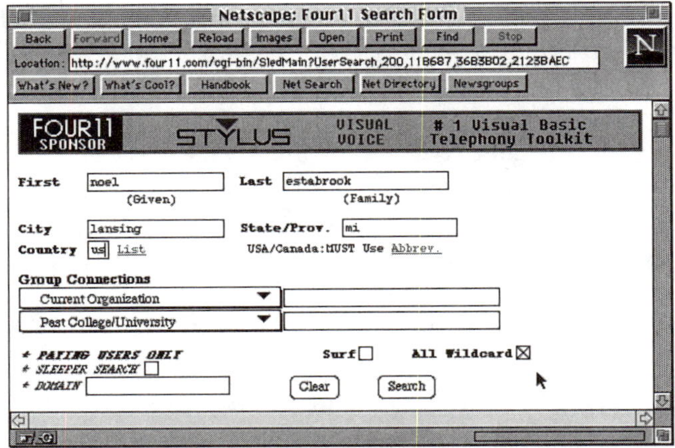

FIGURE 11.4 A typical Four11 search.

Four11 then lists any hits (see Figure 11.5).

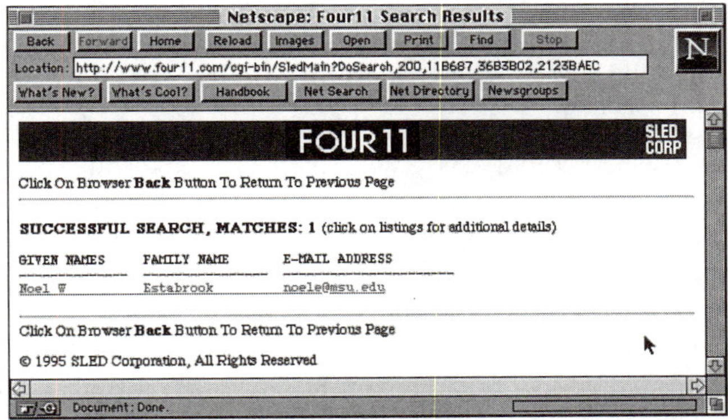

FIGURE 11.5 Four11 search results.

In this lesson, you learned different ways to search for someone's e-mail address. In the next lesson, you learn how to find cool new sites on the World Wide Web.

SEARCHING FOR NEW & COOL WEB SITES

In this lesson, you learn how to locate many of the cool new Web sites on the World Wide Web.

Trying to guess how many new Web pages pop up every month is almost like trying to guess how many babies are born every day—a daunting task. Many estimate that thousands of new Web pages are created every week. Trying to find them, much less figuring out which ones are interesting, is next to impossible.

Fortunately, there are ways to get information about new and interesting Web pages. Some organizations devote both time and resources to keeping up with new and exciting developments on the Web; Netscape is one of them.

Netscape provides two directory buttons, **What's New?** and **What's Cool?** You'll use both of them in this lesson.

WHAT'S NEW?

Netscape has a Web page set up specifically to guide you to new Web pages. It's easy to use and always has something different to offer.

1. Click the What's New? directory button to get to the What's New Web page (see Figure 12.1).
2. Scroll down the page to see what's new on the Web today.

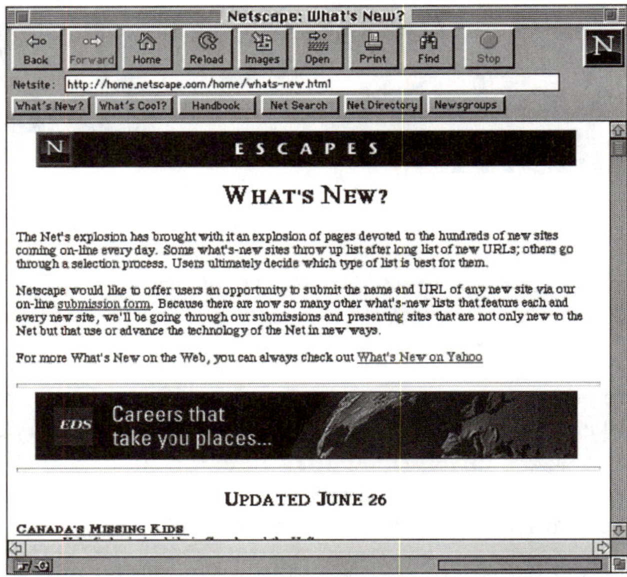

FIGURE 12.1 Netscape's What's New Web page.

Where Are They Now? No doubt, the Web pages you are looking at today will be totally different than the ones that were around when this book was written. Remember, things do change incredibly fast on the Net.

One site that *is* likely to be a constant on Netscape's What's New? page is the **What's New on Yahoo** link. You looked at Yahoo's search page in Lesson 10. Now you're going to look at its directory of what's new on the Web. After you've explored some of the new sites on Netscape's What's New? page:

1. Scroll back up to the top of the page or click the What's New? button again.
2. Click the What's New on Yahoo link. This takes you to the What's New on Yahoo page (see Figure 12.2).

3. As you can see, Yahoo keeps a listing of pages added to its database for the previous week, arranged by date. Select any or all of the date links to take a look at some of the new pages recently posted on the Yahoo database.

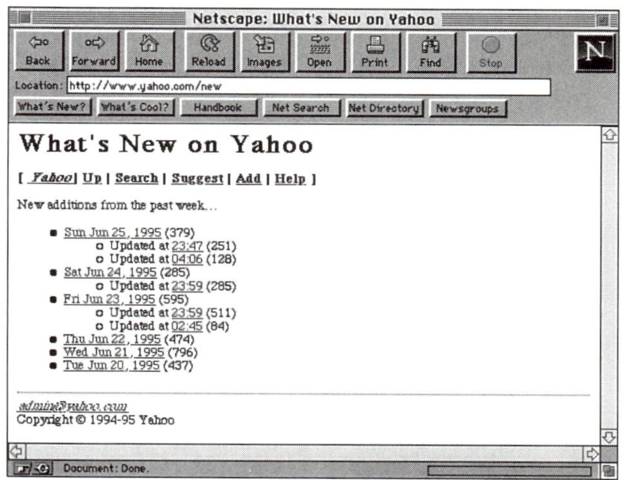

Figure 12.2 What's New on Yahoo page.

As with the What's New? page in Netscape, you simply click the links to find out what's new. However, Yahoo has an added feature that is worth looking at.

Yahoo allows you to search its database of new sites. For instance, what if you want to know if there's anything out there on the latest hot movie? Let's find out:

1. Click the Search link at the top of the Yahoo page.
2. Type the word (or words) you're looking for in the search field pictured in Figure 12.3 and click the Search button.

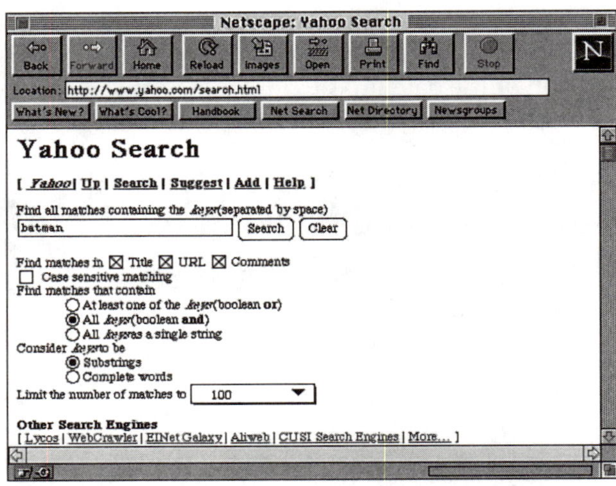

FIGURE 12.3 The Yahoo Search page.

As you can see, Yahoo offers quite a few options to help you in your search. You can look specifically for titles, URLs, or even comments while still conducting AND searches. You can even tell Yahoo how many hits you want to find. A complete description of search options is in Table 12.1.

TABLE 12.1 YAHOO SEARCH OPTIONS

OPTION	DESCRIPTION
Search Field	Type what you're looking for here.
Search button	Begins the search.
Clear button	Clears search information to begin a new search from scratch.
Find matches in	Allows you to find hits in a listing's Title, URL, or Comments. Pick any or all options.

Option	Description
Find matches that contain	For search terms that contain more than one word; **or** returns hits that match either word, **and** returns hits that match both, and **All** matches all characters in a large search term.
Consider keys to be	Tells Yahoo whether you want your terms to be considered small portions of a larger term (substrings) or complete words as typed (words).
Limit the number of matches to	Lets you determine how many hits you wish to see.

Just to give you an idea of how fast the Web works, this search for **batman** was conducted a mere one week after the movie's debut. At that time, Yahoo found 16 Web pages that contained information on the newest Batman movie, *Batman Forever* (see Figure 12.4).

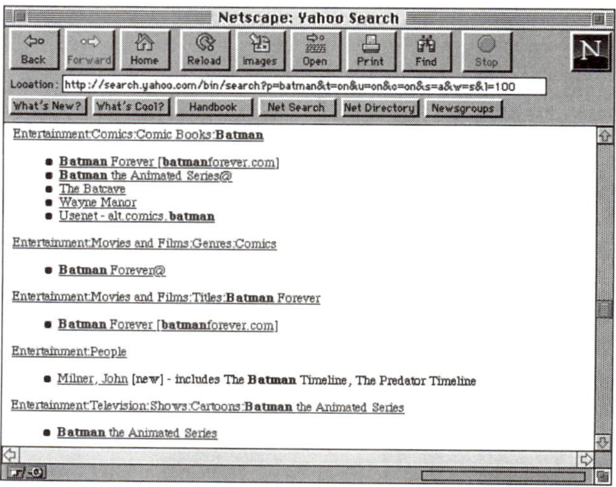

Figure 12.4 Yahoo What's New search results.

WHAT'S COOL?

As you looked through many of the new sites, some contained valuable information, a few may have piqued your interest, and a couple might have even been fun. But let's face it, there were some losers among those winners, too.

That's why you're going to look at the What's Cool? link. These are the "happening" places on the Web—radical, different, interesting, the kind of things that convince you that computer people really *don't* have a life! To help you find them, Netscape has again taken the initiative.

Next to the **What's New?** directory button, you'll notice the **What's Cool?** button:

1. Click the What's Cool? button. This takes you to Netscape's What's Cool? page (see Figure 12.5).

   The sites on the What's Cool? page are more numerous than those on the What's New? page. They also change less often. Several sites that you might want to look at (with their URL in parentheses in case they're gone by the time you read this) are listed at the end of this lesson. Let's look at one in particular right now.

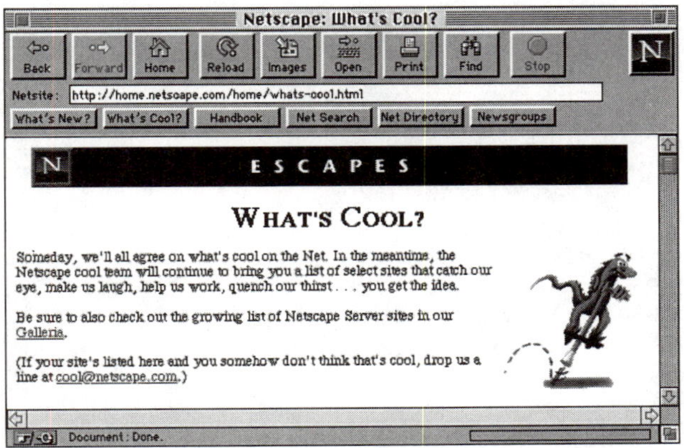

FIGURE 12.5 Netscape's What's Cool? page.

2. Scroll down to and click the Kodak link. This takes you to Kodak's home page (see Figure 12.6).

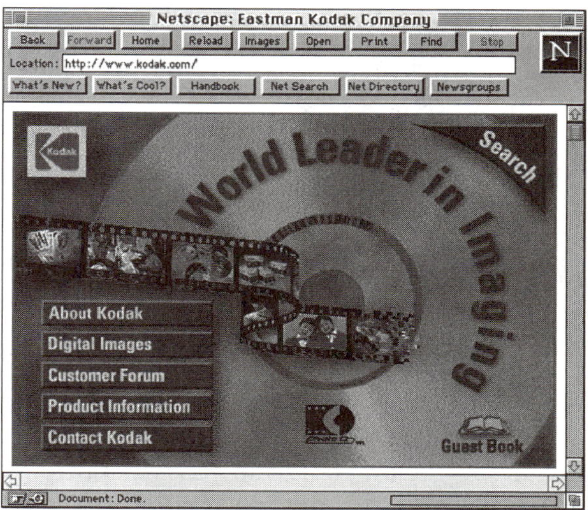

Figure 12.6 The Kodak home page.

3. From here, click the Digital Images button.
4. Next, click the Sample Digital Images button.
5. You are then given a list of image types. Click the Existing Light option.
6. You can now click any image you want to view. Figure 12.7 shows the Existing Light image choices.

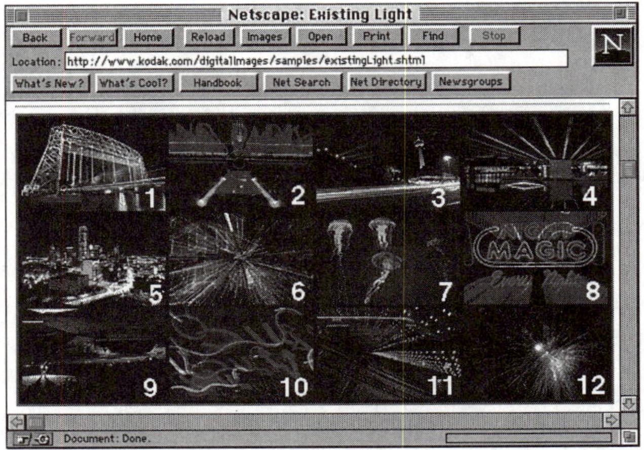

FIGURE 12.7 Existing Light Images.

If you would like to explore some other cool sites before you move on to the next lesson, you might want to check out:

- The 48th Cannes International Film Festival

  http://www.interactive8.com.80/cannes/welcome/welcome.html

- Hitchcock—The Master of Suspense

  http://nextdch.mty.itesm.mx/~plopesa/Kaplan/Hitchcock.html

- United States Central Intelligence Agency

  http://www.odci.gov/

- Random Lightbulb Joke (a new one every 10 seconds)

  http://www.crc.ricoh.com/~marcush/lightbulb/random.cgi

In this lesson, you learned how to find out what's new and what's cool on the Web. In the next lesson, you learn how to access Gopher servers on the Internet.

Accessing Gopher Servers

In this lesson, you learn how to access Gopher servers using Netscape.

What Is a Gopher Server?

Imagine taking a long trip and staying at a Holiday Inn every night. They're nice, but there are other lodgings available. How about spending a couple of nights at a camp site? Ever thought of taking a travel trailer for a week? How about a bed and breakfast for two?

Well, so far you have traveled to many places on the Internet. Up to this point, however, every place you've visited has been the same type of place—a Web page. Are there any other types of places out there on the Internet? Of course there are, and with the help of Netscape, you can go to them.

One of these is Gopher—perhaps you've heard of it? Gopher was first created at the University of Minnesota, the home of the Golden Gophers and was so named because it allows you to "go-fer" information.

If you haven't heard of Gopher before (or even if you have), a brief explanation of what it does might be helpful. Gopher was around long before the Web. As a result, its interface isn't quite as nice—no pictures to look at, no sounds to hear. Basically, Gopher is made up of a series of menus, with each menu leading to other menus, documents, or files. But wait! That doesn't mean there isn't some great stuff out there in Gopherspace.

Gopherspace Gopherspace is the term used to represent all of the Gopher servers in the world. Much like the Web, all of these servers are available and have their own place on the Internet.

Because Gopher has been around so long, the amount of information available through Gopher is significant and continues to be a good source for all types of resources. Luckily for you, all of Gopherspace is available through Netscape.

USING NETSCAPE TO BROWSE GOPHERS

Because Netscape is graphical in nature, even a non-graphical medium like Gopher is spiced up a little. If you were to actually use a Gopher in its natural state, you would navigate numbered menus by using your keyboard.

Netscape, however, places an icon before each Gopher item to help identify it. If you are familiar with these icons, you will navigate better through Gopherspace. Here is a brief explanation of what each icon represents:

ICON	DESCRIPTION
Menu	The folder icon represents another menu. Clicking this icon takes you to another menu with more items; this menu can be on the same Gopher or can link to a Gopher on a different server.
Text	The document icon indicates a text file. These files can be read or downloaded to your machine.

continues

continued

Icon		Description
	Binary file	The 010 document icon represents a binary (non-text) file. (A binary file is comprised of machine code that can't be read as text.) These files are usually graphics, sound files, or software applications that cannot be viewed as text. These types of files usually appear on FTP sites (you will learn about FTP sites in Lesson 14).
	Telnet	The computer icon represents a Telnet session. A *Telnet session* is a way of connecting to another computer that isn't accessible via the Web. For instance, some libraries keep their holdings in a database that is accessible only via Telnet.
	Gopher search	The binocular icon indicates an item that allows you to search for something on Gopher. A Gopher search on Netscape looks very similar to some of the searches you've conducted in earlier lessons. A Gopher search will be demonstrated for you in this lesson.

Now that you know some of the Gopher nuts and bolts, let's see what Gopher can do. For this lesson, let's go to the mother of all Gophers at the University of Minnesota:

1. Using the method you prefer, type **gopher://gopher.micro.umn.edu**. When Netscape has found the University of Minnesota's Gopher, your screen should look like Figure 13.1.
2. Click the Fun & Games link.
3. Next, click the Movies link. Your screen should now look like that shown in Figure 13.2.

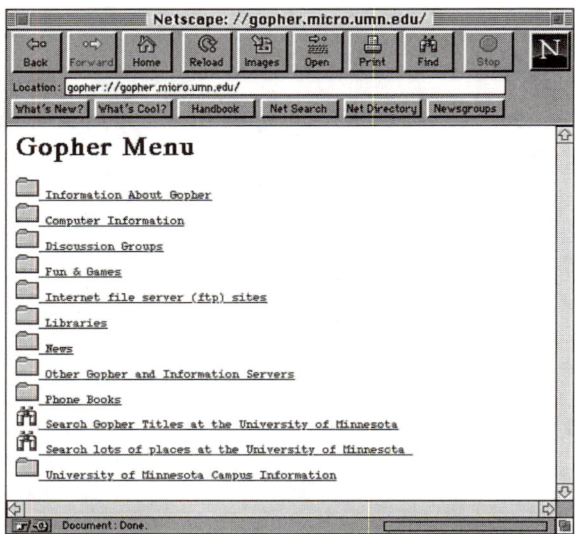

FIGURE 13.1 The University of Minnesota's Gopher.

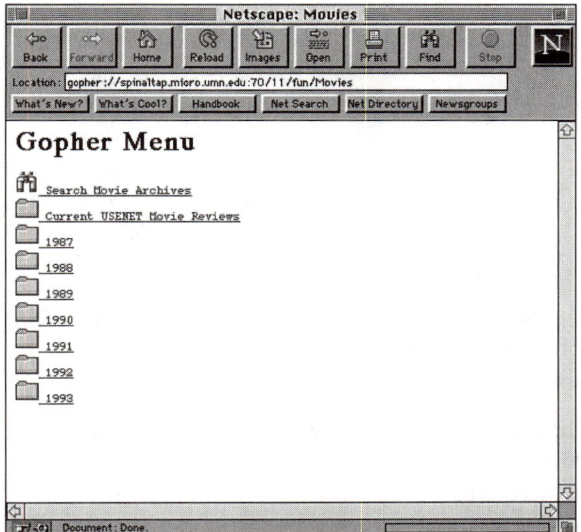

FIGURE 13.2 The University of Minnesota's movie Gopher.

4. Now click Current USENET Movie Reviews. Your screen should show a listing of movie reviews like those pictured in Figure 13.3.

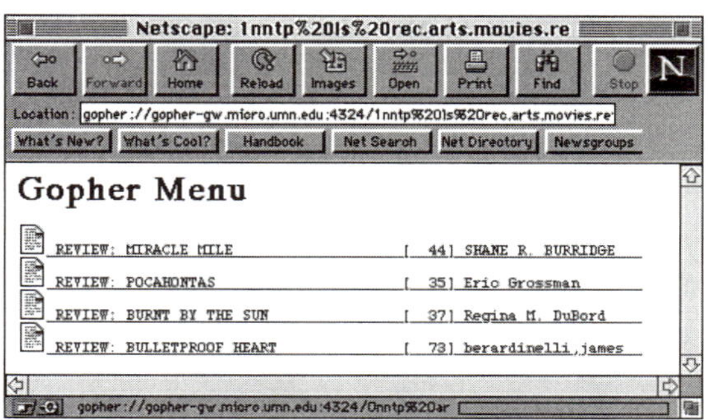

FIGURE 13.3 Current UseNet Movie Reviews.

Feel free to browse around the movie reviews. See what's there, read a few, and see if you agree with them!

4324/1nntp%20ls%20? This isn't the first time it's happened; you click a link and an apparently nonsense string of characters appears in the Location field (see Figure 13.3). These characters usually indicate some computer code that's being used to locate a resource. In this case, Gopher is looking for a UseNet news server (**nntp**) on another computer.

After you have read the Internet's version of Siskel and Ebert, it's time to learn a little more about Gopher.

1. First, use your Back button (or the History feature) to return to the menu shown in Figure 13.2.
2. Click the Search Movie Archives link.
3. A new search page appears. Click in the **Keywords** field, type **clint eastwood**, and press Return (see Figure 13.4).

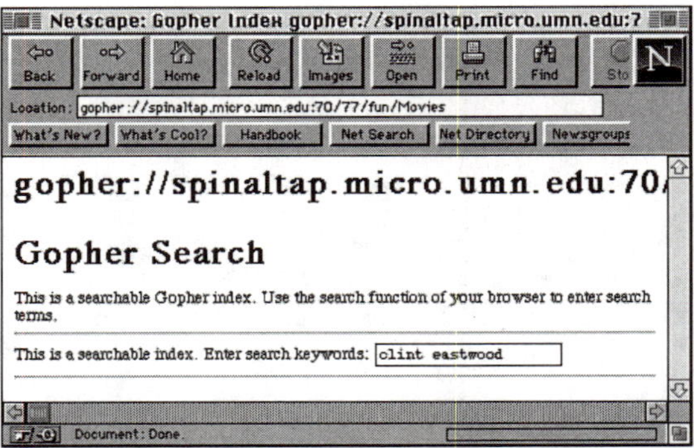

FIGURE 13.4 A typical Gopher search.

The results of your search will show reviews that go all the way back to 1987.

Another thing you will notice almost immediately is that there are movies listed that have nothing to do with Clint Eastwood. For instance, the third item on the list, **The Unbearable Lightness of Being**, was a movie in which Eastwood never appeared or directed. So what's it doing in there? Well, let's use some of the skills learned in a previous lesson to find out:

1. Click the fun/Movies/1988/Mar/THE UNBEARABLE LIGHTNESS OF BEING-1 : From: le link. This takes you to the review.
2. Now click the Find button.
3. Type in **eastwood** and click the Find button.

As you can see, the reviewer mentioned Clint Eastwood in reference to his relationship to the director of *The Unbearable Lightness of Being* (see Figure 13.5).

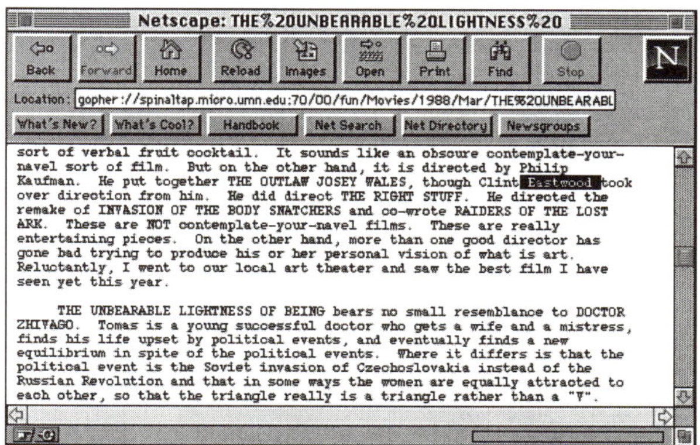

FIGURE 13.5 An unintentional reference to Eastwood in an otherwise unrelated film.

In this lesson, you learned how to use Netscape to "go-fer" information using Gopher. In the next lesson, you learn how to use Netscape to get resources using FTP.

Accessing FTP Sites

In this lesson, you learn how to use Netscape to access FTP sites on the Internet.

What Is FTP?

In the last lesson, you discovered that Netscape can give you access to more than just Web pages. You learned about Gopher, which is a text-based repository of files and other resources organized into a system of menus.

FTP sites are similar to Gopher sites in that they contain information that is organized into menus. Also, when accessed by Netscape, an FTP server looks very similar to a Gopher server.

FTP FTP stands for *File Transfer Protocol*. This is one of the oldest standards on the Internet and has been around as long as the Internet has been in existence. Computers use FTP to communicate with each other and exchange files and other resources.

But that's where the similarities end. First, the menus in FTP are referred to as *directories*. Second, FTP directories aren't often labeled with recognizable English words, but sometimes appear to be titled in hieroglyphics. (See Table 14.1 for a list of some of the more common directories in FTP and what they contain.) Lastly, FTP sites primarily carry *binary files* that usually represent actual software applications or formatted text files.

Formatted Text Any time you use a word processor, code that you don't see is inserted into the document. This code can make text **bold**, *italicized*, or do a hundred other things. This code is usually referred to as formatting.

Table 14.1 Common Directory Names on FTP Sites

Directory name	Full name	Description
/app or /apps	Applications	Generally consists of computer applications of various types.
/comm or /cmp	Communications	Contains communications software such as Gopher clients, FTP clients, and so on.
/comp	Compression	Usually contains compression programs such as Compact-Pro or Stuffit Lite.
/dev	Development	Contains programs for software developers; rarely useful to recreational computer users.
/game	Games	Does this really need an explanation?
/grf	Graphics	Consists of files that have to do with graphics, including actual pictures, picture display programs, and the like.

continues

TABLE 14.1 CONTINUED

DIRECTORY NAME	FULL NAME	DESCRIPTION
/pub	Public	This is usually the main public directory; it often acts as the root directory for software and files downloadable by users.
/util	Utilities	Contains that subgroup of programs that do highly specialized tasks. Often includes Extensions or Control Panels. Can also represent a directory with specific types of utilities. For instance, /graphicutils contains graphic utilities.
/vir	Virus	Contains Virus detection and elimination software.

Anonymous FTP sites are commonly used by computer hardware and software companies to distribute applications and software updates to their customers. In fact, you probably got the copy of Netscape you are running now off the Netscape FTP site.

Anonymous FTP Generally, you need some type of ID and password to log in to another computer. However, if each FTP site required different IDs and passwords for each user, FTP would be useless. To solve this problem, many sites allow you to log in with the ID *anonymous.* You can then supply your e-mail address as a password and take advantage of all FTP has to offer. When you use Netscape, you won't need to worry about supplying an ID or password; Netscape does it for you.

ACCESSING FTP SERVERS

To jump to an FTP site, you can either click an FTP link or enter its URL in the Location field. There is one slight difference in how you enter an FTP URL.

You've no doubt noticed that all Web addresses begin with **http://**. In the last lesson, you learned that Gopher addresses begin with **gopher://**. Well, you guessed it, FTP addresses begin with **ftp://**. Let's take a look at Netscape's FTP server:

1. Using your preferred method, go to **ftp://ftp.netscape.com**. This takes you to the Netscape FTP site pictured in Figure 14.1.

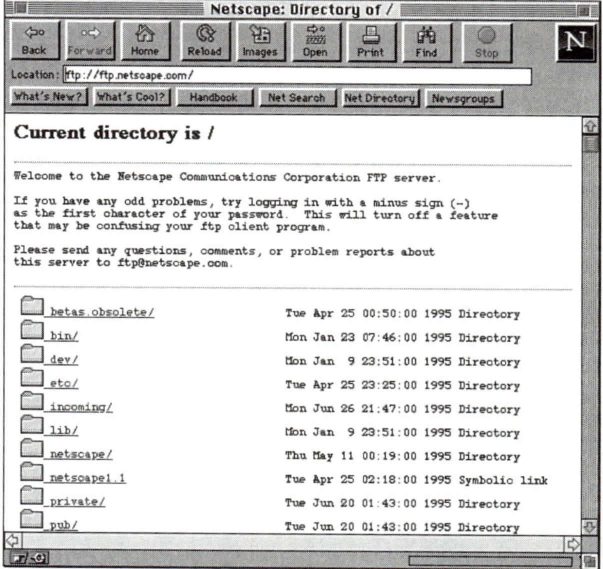

FIGURE 14.1 Netscape's FTP site.

2. Scroll down the page until you can see the complete directory listing.

More Than One Way... Like every other popular place on the Net, Netscape's FTP site can get rather busy. To alleviate this problem, Netscape has set up alternate FTP sites for you to access at **ftp://ftp2.netscape.com** and **ftp://ftp3.netscape.com**.

Netscape uses icons to clue you in as to what you're seeing on FTP sites, just as it does on Gopher sites. Many of these icons are the same as those found in Gopher; some are different.

ICON	DESCRIPTION
Directory	The folder icon represents a directory or subdirectory.
Document	The file icon indicates a document containing text. Many times, there will be a description of the type of text file next to the file name (see Figure 14.2).
Generic file	A blank file icon can represent a compressed executable file or some type of file Netscape doesn't recognize.
Binary file	The 010 icon usually represents an executable program.
Graphic file	The image icon indicates a graphic file that Netscape recognizes.

NAVIGATING THROUGH AN FTP SERVER

FTP sites are made up of directories and subdirectories, much like those on your Macintosh. Just as opening a folder on your Macintosh reveals more folders, documents, and files, so too does clicking a folder in Netscape. For instance, from the top-level directory in Netscape:

1. Click the Netscape1.1 link.
2. Next, click the mac link. This takes you to the directory that contains version 1.1 of Netscape Navigator (see Figure 14.2). Notice that the name of each folder you've clicked has been added to the URL in the Location field.

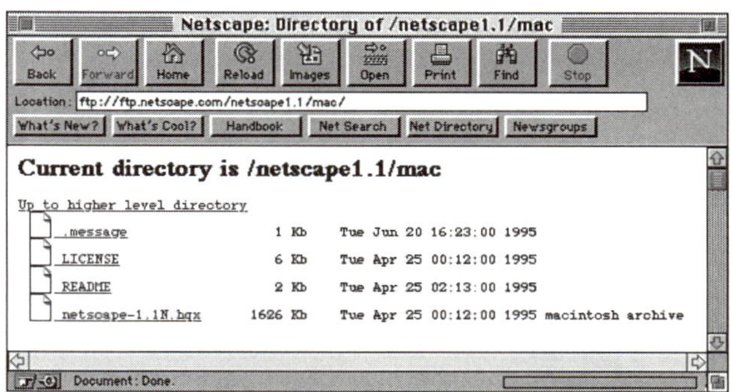

FIGURE 14.2 Netscape Navigator 1.1 directory.

In this lesson, you learned how to access FTP sites. In the next lesson, you learn how to locate and transfer files to your computer from FTP sites.

Finding and Downloading Files from FTP Sites

In this lesson, you learn how to use Netscape to find and transfer files to your computer from an FTP site.

Locating Anonymous FTP Servers

If the amount of information available on FTP is anything like what's available on the Web and Gopher (and it is), it would be helpful to have a tool to help you find it. Enter Archie.

Archie is basically a service that helps you locate files all over the Internet. Archie accomplishes this by constantly updating a database that contains information on files all over the world. This server is then available for you to use to find the files you want.

To begin your FTP search, you need to jump to a Web page that has links to Archie sites worldwide.

1. Using your preferred method, type **http://web.nexor.co.uk/archie.html**. This takes you to Nexor's list of WWW Archie Services (see Figure 15.1).
2. Scroll down and select an Archie server of your choice. For this lesson, click the AA at NCSA link. When you do, you'll see an Archie search form.
3. Enter the name of the file you wish to find. If you're not sure of the name, you can enter the first few letters of the file name and Archie will try to find it. For this example, you'll look for a handy utility called TechTool, so type **techtool** as the file you'd like to search for.
4. In the **Types of Search** field, select Case Insensitive Substring Match. You will generally want your searches to

be case-insensitive so that you'll have a better chance of finding what you're looking for.

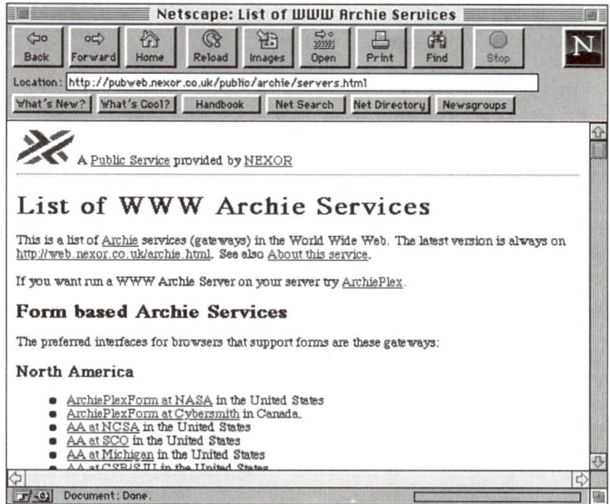

FIGURE 15.1 List of WWW Archie Services.

5. Decide how you want the search results sorted. Often, newer versions will appear at the top of your hit list if you choose sort By Date.

6. Decide how much impact you want to place on other users (in other words, how much of *their* search time you want to take up) who are also conducting searches. The nicer you are, the longer your search will take.

7. When deciding to use other Archie servers, you may have to experiment with this setting to see which selection produces the best search results. For this example, try Canada.

8. The default number of file locations returned is 10. You may want to make this number a little higher. Remember, the higher the number, the longer the search will take. Your search form should now look like Figure 15.2.

9. Click the Submit button to begin your search. In a few moments, the results of your search will be displayed (see Figure 15.3).

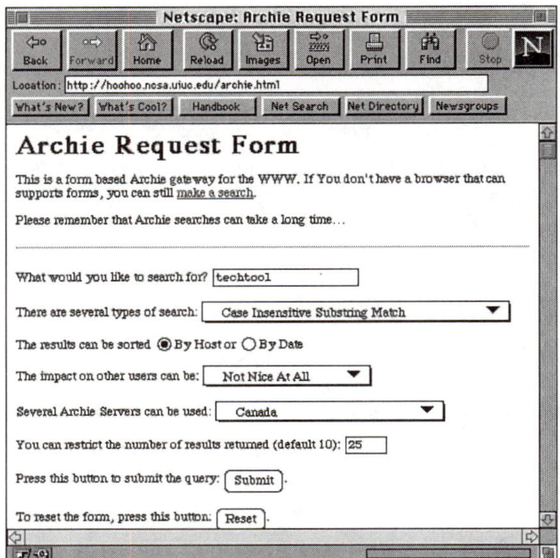

FIGURE 15.2 Completed Archie search form.

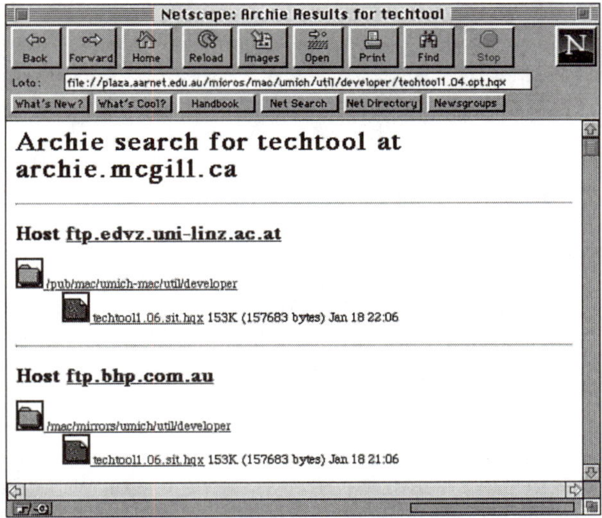

FIGURE 15.3 Results of Archie search.

Now that you have found a file you want, you are ready to learn how to download it to your computer.

TRANSFERRING A FILE FROM AN FTP SERVER

Once you've found a file you'd like to have, either by browsing or using Archie, you are ready to transfer it to your machine.

Virus Alert! Don't press the panic button just yet, but be aware that when you transfer a file from an FTP site, you are potentially exposing your computer to viruses. Most FTP sites are clean, but an occasional virus will get through. Always make sure you are running an up-to-date anti-virus program before you begin downloading files.

First, you must tell Netscape where to download files on your computer:

1. Open the Options menu and choose the Preferences option.
2. At the top of the Preferences dialog box, there is a pop-up menu. Select the Applications and Directories option. Your dialog box should now look like Figure 15.4.
3. Netscape downloads files to your Temporary Directory. In the **Directories** area of the Preferences dialog box, click the Browse button and then select the directory you would like to use.

On the Desktop You might want to have Netscape download files to your desktop at first. This way, you can see what you're getting immediately. This allows you to play with, move, or delete any downloaded files quickly and easily.

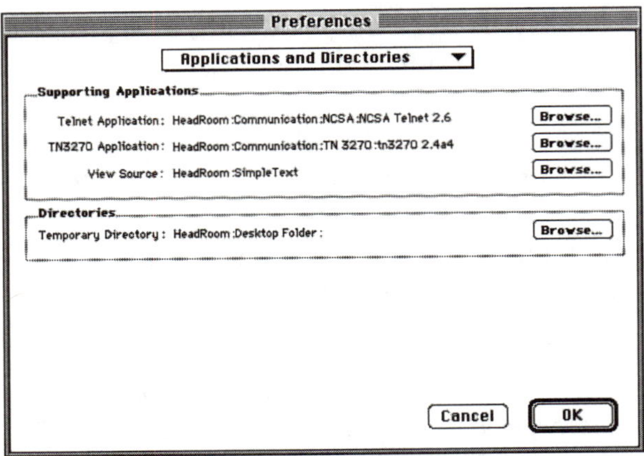

FIGURE 15.4 The Applications and Directories Preferences dialog box.

4. After you've selected the directory of your choice, click the OK button.

There is one more thing you need before you can begin downloading files, however; you will need to get a copy of a *Helper Application*.

Helper Application A helper application is any piece of software that helps another application become more functional. In this instance, you will make use of a compression program to "help" Netscape decompress programs that it would not normally be able to.

Many Macintosh files you find on FTP sites end in the file extension HQX or SIT. These extensions indicate that the file has been compressed to save space on the FTP site. To decompress files of this type, you need a utility such as Stuffit Expander or Stuffit Lite. If you do not already have an operational copy of Stuffit Expander or Stuffit Lite installed, you will need to get one now.

The Chicken or the Egg? There may be a slight problem getting a copy of one of these utilities. You see, even though they're available via FTP, Netscape can't download them in a format that your computer can use. To get these utilities, you need to contact your system administrator or Internet Service Provider; they should be able to get you a copy or tell you where to get one. If worse comes to worse, you can contact the makers of Stuffit at:

Aladdin Systems, Inc.
165 Westridge Dr.
WatsonVille, CA 95076
Voice: (408)761-6200
Fax: (408)761-6206

aladdin@well.com

If you have a different FTP application that will translate these files, you can get a copy of Stuffit Expander at **ftp://ftp.ncsa.uiuc.edu/Mac/Mosaic/Helpers/**.

After one of these utilities has been installed on your computer, you can proceed to tell Netscape how to use it:

1. In the Preferences dialog box, choose Helper Applications in the pop-up menu.
2. Click the New button for the new setting.
3. A new dialog box appears. Click in the **Mime Type** field and type **application**.
4. Click in the **Mime Subtype** field and type **mac-binhex40**. Your dialog box should look like Figure 15.5. Click the OK button.

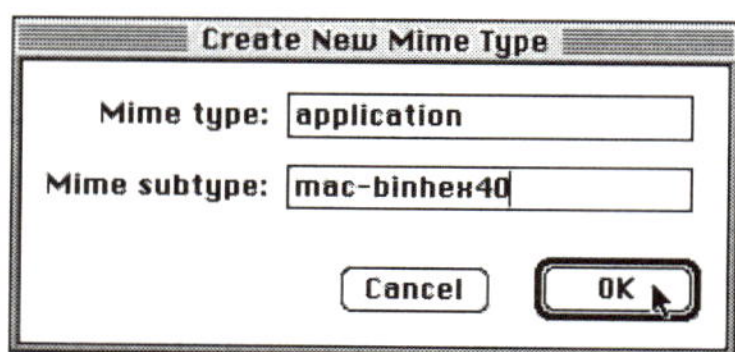

FIGURE 15.5 The Create New Mime Type dialog box.

5. When you return to the Preferences dialog box, click in the **Extensions** field and type **hqx**.

6. Click the Browse button next to **Application Unknown**. In the new dialog box that appears, find and then choose Stuffit Expander (or Stuffit Lite).

7. Now click the Launch Application radio button next to **Action**. When you have done this, your dialog box should look like Figure 15.6. Click the OK button and you're done.

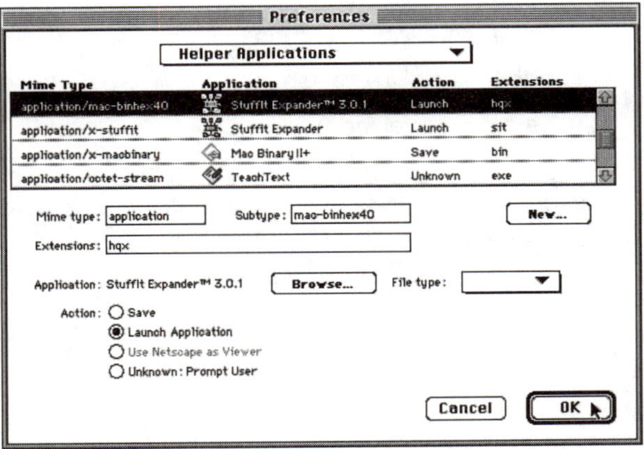

FIGURE 15.6 The completed Helper Applications Preferences dialog box.

If you would also like to set up Netscape to handle SIT files, simply repeat steps 2-6 above. In Steps 4 and 5 however, enter **x-stuffit** and **sit** instead of **mac-binhex40** and **hqx**.

Remember that utility you found a while ago? Finally, you are ready to download it. Simply click any of the techtool links Archie located for you and wait for it to download. If you run into a busy site, pick another one until you find one that downloads.

Of course, you may not always download files that have resulted from an Archie search. In this case, you need to go to an FTP site, navigate through the directories, and then click the file you want. For instance, if you want to download an anti-virus utility:

1. Using your preferred method, go to **ftp://yuma.acns.colostate.edu/**.
2. Click the software.mac directory link.
3. At the next screen, click the virus directory link.
4. Now click the first item labeled disinfectant34.sea. This is the file you want.

Save Some Time To save some time downloading the file, if you already know the file's name and location, include it in the URL that you enter in the Location field. For example, you could have typed:

> **ftp://yuma.acns.colostate.edu/software.mac/virus/disinfectant34.sea.hqx**

in the Location field and the file would have immediately downloaded to your machine.

In this lesson, you learned how to find and transfer files using FTP. In the next lesson, you learn how to access newsgroups using Netscape.

Lesson 16 Accessing UseNet Newsgroups

In this lesson, you learn how to use Netscape to access UseNet newsgroups.

What Are UseNet Newsgroups?

Newsgroups are basically electronic discussion groups. People in UseNet newsgroups discuss topics ranging from aviation to zoology. There are currently over 10,000 newsgroups that can be read across the world. There are thousands more that can only be read locally.

UseNet The term UseNet predates the Internet and refers to an early system of connecting mainframe computers using standard telephone lines and crude versions of desktop modems to transfer discussion articles.

Typically, newsgroups are designed to cover one topic. For instance, the group comp.sys.mac.apps is a group for discussion of COMPuter SYStems with a focus on MACintosh APPlicationS. Despite the fact that these groups *should* discuss one topic, this often isn't the case.

For example, there is inevitably some person who feels the need to discuss the superiority of PCs over Macs on the comp.sys.mac.apps group. These off-topic posts often degenerate into mudslinging sessions (called *flame wars* on the Net) that are sometimes annoying and often downright offensive. Despite this, most discussion on UseNet is relatively cordial and provides good information to users.

CONFIGURING NETSCAPE FOR NEWSGROUPS

To really get a feel for what newsgroups are and which ones might be of interest to you, you need to look at some of them. Before you do, however, you need to tell Netscape where to look to find these newsgroups.

1. Open the Options menu and choose the Preferences option.
2. In the Preferences dialog box, select the Mail and News option from the pop-up menu at the top. When you do, your dialog box will look like Figure 16.1.

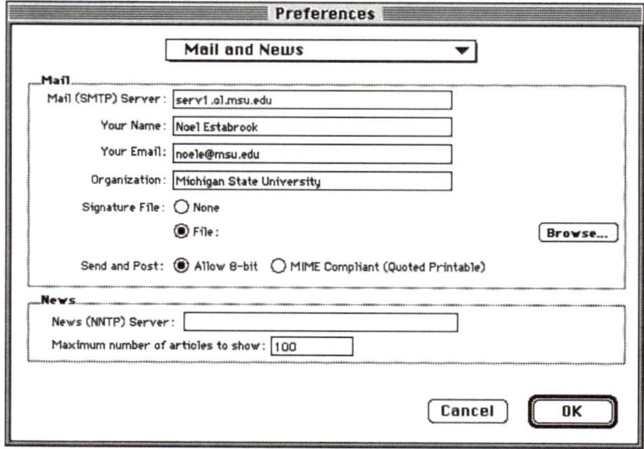

FIGURE 16.1 Mail and News Preferences dialog box.

3. In the News (NNTP) Server field, enter the name of your news server. If you're not sure of the address of your news server, contact your System Administrator or Internet Service Provider (ISP).

Tell Netscape Who You Are Because posting to newsgroups is effective only if Netscape knows who you are, you should also take a moment to fill in the Mail information. Your Name, SMTP Server, E-mail address, and Organization should be filled in. As with the News Server, if you don't know the address of your SMTP (Simple Mail Transfer Protocol) server address, contact your System Administrator or ISP.

4. Click the OK button to save your changes.

Accessing Newsgroups

You are now ready to use newsgroups. To access newsgroups:

1. Click the Newsgroups directory button at the top of Netscape's window. If you have more than one news server, Netscape first lets you choose which one you want to use. If you only have access to one news server, this screen does not appear.
2. If you have a choice of servers, click the server name you entered in the Preferences dialog box. This takes you to a listing of newsgroups (see Figure 16.2). Netscape automatically subscribes you to three newsgroups:
    - news.announce.newusers
    - news.newusers.questions
    - news.answers

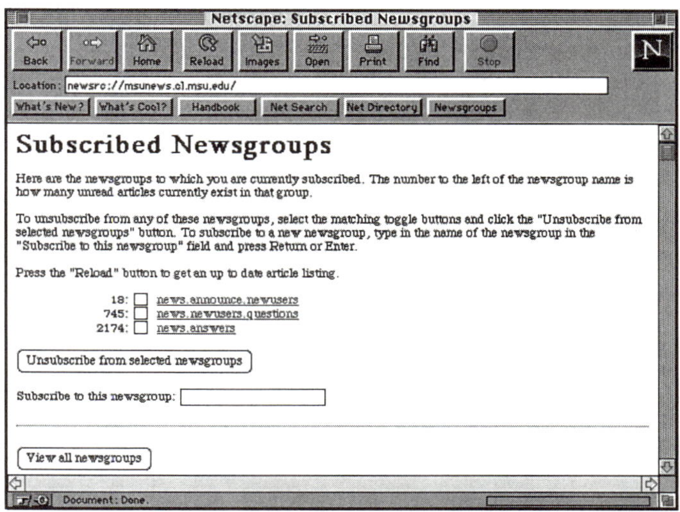

FIGURE 16.2 Initial newsgroup listing.

You may want to browse these three groups for a while to get a feel for what UseNet newsgroups are all about. All three groups deal with topics that new users may want to know about. If you don't want to continue subscribing to these newsgroups, simply select the check box next to each one you wish to unsubscribe to and click the Unsubscribe from selected newsgroups button. Keep in mind, you haven't learned how to subscribe to newsgroups yet—that comes in the next lesson.

Subscribe/Unsubscribe In some sense, newsgroups can be thought of as interactive magazines. As you know, before you can receive a magazine at home, you must first subscribe to it. In the same way, when you know longer wish to receive the magazine, you tell them you wish to unsubscribe. This process is the same for newsgroups, except it's all done online.

3. To see the other newsgroups available, scroll down to the View all newsgroups button and click it. This lists all of

the newsgroups available to you (see Figure 16.3). If your news server carries a lot of groups, this might take a few minutes, so be patient.

FIGURE 16.3 A typical newsgroup list.

Your News List Looks Different? Because each news server is different, the way in which newsgroups are arranged on each server might also be different. Factors such as the number of groups and manner of grouping can affect how the groups look to you.

You are now ready to proceed to the next lesson. Don't allow yourself to be confused by the apparent nonsensical arrangement and naming of what we've promised are in fact newsgroups. Hold on to your hats—we ain't done yet!

In this lesson, you learned how to configure Netscape for newsgroups and how to access newsgroups on your news server. In the next lesson, you learn how to read and respond to news items and how to subscribe to newsgroups.

Using Newsgroups

LESSON 17

In this lesson, you learn about using newsgroups—how to subscribe to, read, and post news items to newsgroups.

Subscribing to Newsgroups

Your first task in beginning to use newsgroups is to subscribe to some groups. Before you do, however, perhaps a little explanation might help you understand how newsgroups are organized. Most of the major newsgroups are grouped into one of the seven major *hierarchies* listed below:

- **alt.* (alternative)** The alt category contains groups that can't be easily categorized into any other mainstream hierarchy.
- **comp.* (computers)** This category contains newsgroups about computers and computer science.
- **news.*** This hierarchy contains groups that discuss news about newsgroups and their operations.
- **rec.* (recreational)** This is the fun category that deals with recreational interests.
- **sci.* (science)** The issues in this category have to do with science-related fields.
- **soc.* (social)** This hierarchy encompasses all types of social issues.
- **talk.*** This category contains groups designed specifically for debate or conversation.

Hierarchy A hierarchy is really a fancy name for category. However, there are also sub-hierarchies. For instance, there is a broad alt.* hierarchy, but there is also an alt.animals.* hierarchy, and so on. Every time you see a * in a hierarchy, you know that there will be another subset of groups under it.

Look at the hierarchies your news server has, as you did in the last lesson. Notice that there seem to be a lot more than seven categories. That's because many servers also carry many of the minor hierarchies such as biz (business), bionet (biology), misc (miscellaneous), and others. Don't let this bother you; it just means you have more topics to choose from!

You're ready to subscribe to a group, you say? Okay, let's go. First, subscribing to newsgroups ensures that Netscape is able to keep track of newsgroups for you. Which groups you're subscribed to and which articles you've read are just a couple of the things Netscape monitors for you. You'll subscribe to one newsgroup (alt.culture.www) in this lesson. Subscribing to any other group requires the exact same steps.

But I Don't Get alt.* What do you do if your news server doesn't carry the alt.* hierarchy? Well, because the process for subscribing is the same regardless of group, just follow the steps outlined below for a hierarchy of your choice.

To subscribe to a newsgroup:

1. In the main hierarchy window, click the alt.* hierarchy link.
2. Scroll down to the next page until you see the alt.culture.* hierarchy link (aren't you glad these are in alphabetical order?) and click it.
3. On the next screen, scroll down to the bottom until you find the **alt.culture.www** link. Select the check box next to that group by clicking in it (see Figure 17.1).

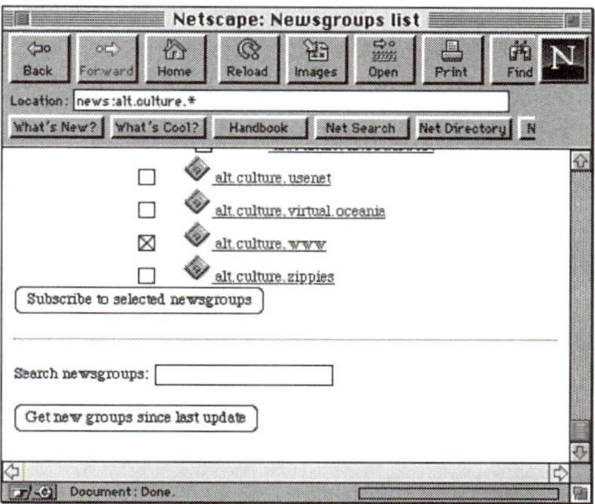

FIGURE 17.1 Subscribing to alt.culture.www.

4. Click the Subscribe to selected newsgroups button. After Netscape subscribes you, the newsgroup appears on your Subscribed Newsgroups list. Your list should now look similar to Figure 17.2. This group remains on your list until you unsubscribe from it.

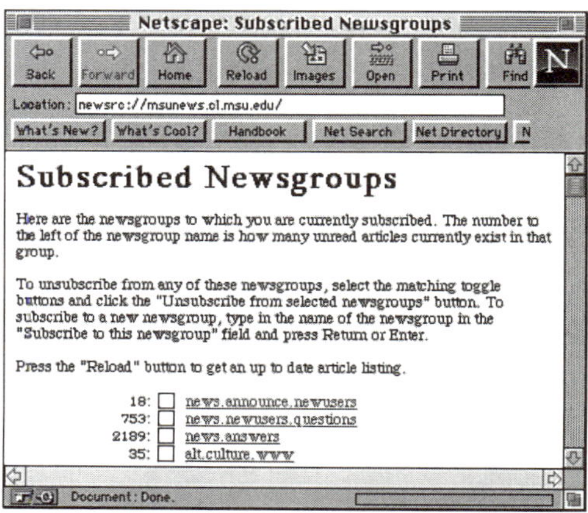

FIGURE 17.2 Subscribed Newsgroups list.

Remember, you can subscribe to as many newsgroups as you like by following the four simple steps above. For now though, let's move on to the rest of the lesson.

READING NEWS ITEMS

Reading articles is really a relatively easy process. To begin, click the alt.culture.www group. Your window will look something like Figure 17.3.

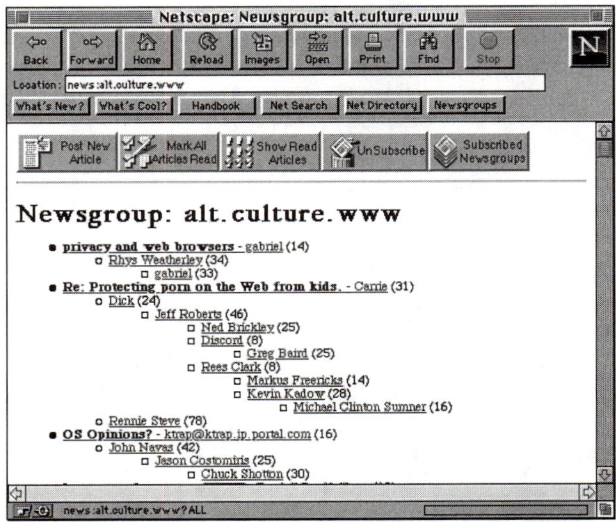

FIGURE 17.3 alt.culture.www articles.

First, it's important to know how articles are organized. On newsgroups, topics are organized into threads. A *thread* is simply a group of articles that has one particular topic in common.

For instance, if you look again at Figure 17.3, you'll notice that there is a thread titled **privacy and web browsers**. Netscape indicates the title and/or the first article in a thread by bold type. Each reply in that thread is indented to various places depending on which article it is replying to. Finally, each article has a number next to it indicating how many lines that particular article has.

To read an article, simply click it. You are now reading a newsgroup article (see Figure 17.4).

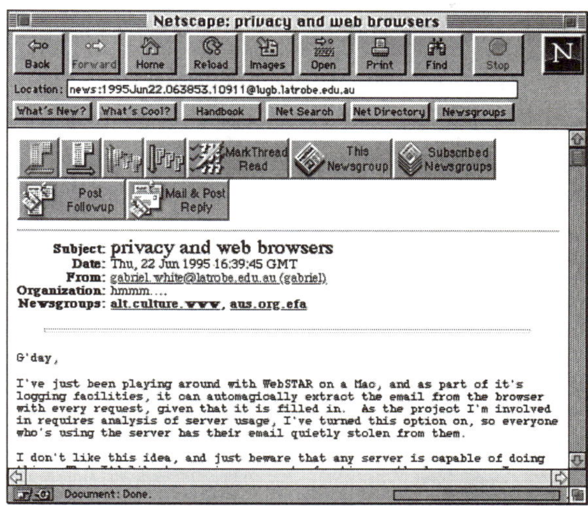

FIGURE 17.4 A typical newsgroup article.

There is, however, a little more to reading articles in newsgroups. Notice that some new buttons appear at the top of an article when you choose to read it. It will help you to know what a few of these buttons mean.

Button	Description
Forward/Back	Clicking these buttons takes you to the next or previous article in a thread.
Next/Previous	Clicking these buttons takes you to the first article in the next or previous thread.
Mark Thread Read	Clicking this button tells Netscape that you don't want to see any of the articles in a particular thread anymore.

Am I the Only Novice? No, you're not. As fast as the Internet is growing, there are *newbies* on the Internet every day. If you read newsgroups enough, you'll realize this. With time, it will be easy to tell the experts from the beginners, and one day, you'll be an expert, too.

Posting News Items

This lesson is also intended to give you a brief overview of how to post articles to newsgroups. At the newsgroup level (the level that shows all of the articles and threads), there is a button titled **Post New Article**. You can click this button to begin composing an article.

You can also reply to posts (and even send personal e-mail replies to posts). You can do this by clicking the Mail & Post Reply button while reading an article. Whichever way you go, you'll end up at the same place (see Figure 17.5).

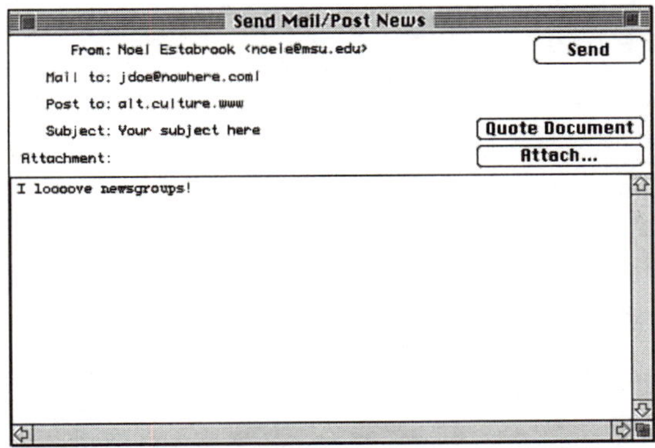

FIGURE 17.5 The Send Mail/Post News window.

Read First It is always recommended that you read a newsgroup for a while before posting or replying. Doing so *can* save you time; becoming familiar with a group lets you post appropriately and, therefore, avoid having to deal with some of the flames talked about in the last chapter.

Depending on whether you're posting a new article, a reply, or e-mail, you'll need to fill in each of the message headings, as well as the body of the message itself. To do so:

1. Fill in the **Mail To**, **Post to**, and **Subject** lines by clicking next to each one and typing in the appropriate information. You'll notice that when you're replying to a post, these areas are already filled in.
2. Click in the box where your message body is to appear. Type in your message.
3. When you are done, click the Send button.

Keep in mind that these two lessons are in no way meant to be an exhaustive treatment of newsgroups. If you want to learn more about newsgroups, refer to Que's *Using UseNet Newsgroups*.

One more note before you leave this lesson. If you plan on using newsgroups on a regular basis, you should consider getting a piece of software that is designed for handling news. Although Netscape is sufficient for the recreational and occasional user, there are many things newsgroups have to offer that Netscape does not take advantage of. An excellent application for reading news on the Macintosh is Newswatcher, which can be found at: **ftp://ftp.acns.nwu.edu/pub/newswatcher/**.

In this lesson, you learned how to subscribe, read, and post to newsgroups. In the next lesson, you learn how to send e-mail using Netscape.

LESSON 18

Sending E-Mail Using Netscape

In this lesson, you learn how to use Netscape to send e-mail to other Internet users.

What Is E-Mail?

E-mail is short for electronic mail. E-mail is still probably the most common use of the Internet today. E-mail can be sent and received very quickly—usually in a matter of seconds or minutes. This has caused frequent Internet users to refer to standard postal mail as "snail mail."

It should be noted at the beginning of this lesson that Netscape is not the best e-mail application available, primarily because Netscape can't receive mail; it can only send. For this reason, it's recommended that you use a client designed specifically for e-mail.

Real E-Mail To really use e-mail effectively, you should not use Netscape. Instead, find an e-mail client such as Eudora. Eudora has a lot of features designed specifically for e-mail. You can get a copy by going to **ftp://ftp.qualcomm.com/quest/eudora/mac/1.5/** and downloading **eudora 153.hqx** (for a standard Macintosh) or **eudora153fat.hqx** (for a PowerMac).

However, there may be times when you will want to send e-mail using Netscape, such as when you run across an e-mail address on a Web site to which you want to quickly send a message. The process for sending e-mail is similar to the one described in Lesson 17.

CONFIGURING NETSCAPE TO SEND E-MAIL

Configuring Netscape for e-mail was briefly covered in Lesson 16. However, if you didn't feel the need to configure Netscape for e-mail at that time, here is a reminder of how to do it:

1. Open the Options menu and choose the Preferences option. The Preferences dialog box appears.
2. Select the Mail and News option from the pop-up menu in the Preferences dialog box.
3. In the **Mail (SMTP) Server** field, enter the name of your local mail server.
4. In the **Your Name** field, enter your name as you want it to appear on e-mail messages.
5. In the **Your Email** field, enter your e-mail address. It should be in the form *userid@mail.server*. For example, the author's e-mail address is noele@msu.edu.
6. In the **Organization** field, enter an (optional) organization name.
7. If you have a **Signature File**, click the Browse button and click your signature file. Lesson 24 covers the signature file more in-depth. When you are done, your preferences should be set similarly to those shown in Figure 18.1.
8. Click OK to close the Preferences dialog box.

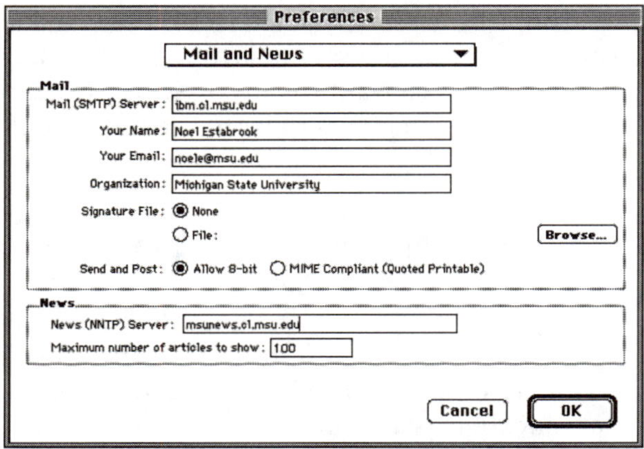

FIGURE 18.1 The completed Mail and News Preferences dialog box.

SENDING E-MAIL

After you have configured Netscape, you are ready to send a message:

1. Open the File menu and choose the Mail Document option. A mail composition window appears (see Figure 18.2).

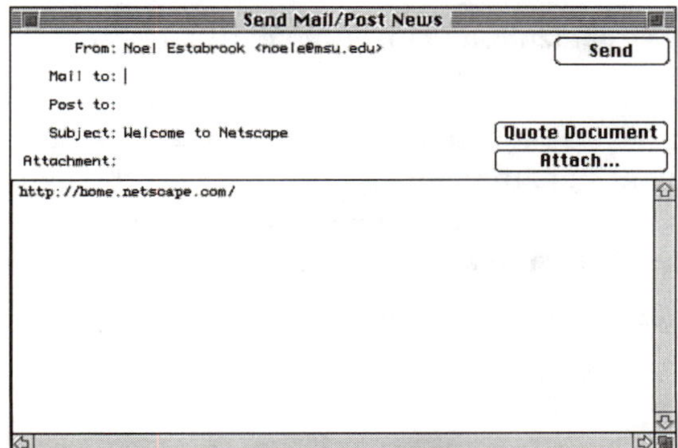

FIGURE 18.2 The e-mail composition window.

2. Enter the e-mail address of the person you want to send your message to in the form *userid@mail.server*. For instance, if you want to send e-mail to the author, you'd enter **noele@msu.edu**.

3. Press the Tab key twice to move to the **Subject** field.

4. In the **Subject** field, enter an optional subject reference. This should give the recipient an idea of what the message is about and should be relatively short.

5. If you're attaching a file to the e-mail message, click the Attach button to open the Attachment dialog box (see Figure 18.3).

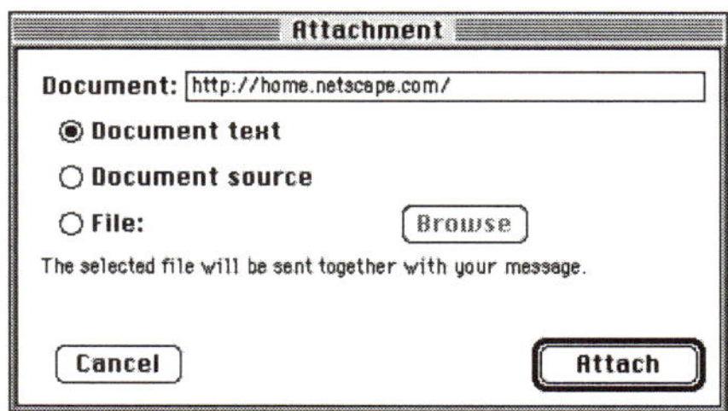

FIGURE 18.3 The Attachment dialog box.

6. If you want to attach only the text on the Web page you're currently reading, select the Document text radio button and click the Attach button.

7. If you want to attach the Web page text, including all of the HTML code on the page, select the Document source radio button and click the Attach button.

8. To attach the file of your choice, select the File radio button, and then click the Browse button. You can then select the file you want to attach by double-clicking it. When you return to the Attachment dialog box, click the Attach button. This returns you to your message window.

9. You can now enter the text of your message in the message field and click the Send button.

In this lesson, you learned how to use Netscape to send e-mail messages. In the next lesson, you learn how to view and save graphics using Netscape.

VIEWING AND SAVING GRAPHICS

In this lesson, you learn how to view and save various types of graphics in Netscape.

NETSCAPE AND GRAPHICS

You've no doubt heard that one of the greatest things about the Web is its ability to display different kinds of media to make it more exciting. Graphics are one of those aspects of the Web that make it like no other place on the Internet. As you've already seen, Netscape allows you to view most graphics with ease.

Occasionally, however, you run across certain types of graphic files that Netscape is not capable of viewing or displaying. Table 19.1 gives some of the most common graphic types:

TABLE 19.1 COMMON GRAPHIC TYPES

ABBREVIATION	FILE EXTENSION	DESCRIPTION
GIF	.gif	Graphics Interchange Format
JPEG	.jpg	Joint Photographics Expert Group
BMP	.bmp	Windows Bitmap Format
PCX	.pcx	Zsoft Paint
PICT	.pic	Standard picture format
TIFF	.tif	Tag Image File Format

There are, of course, hundreds more, but these are some of the standard ones. Ninety-five percent of all of the graphics you see on the Web are in either GIF (pronounced jiff) or JPEG (pronounced jay-peg) format. Fortunately for you, Netscape is configured to view these two file types without the need for any other applications. GIFs and JPEGs are displayed in a Netscape window.

However, the other formats listed above, along with any others you might find on the Web, can't be viewed by Netscape. For these types of graphics, you need to use a helper application.

GETTING HELPER APPLICATIONS

As you learned in Lesson 15, you must first get a copy of a helper application before you can begin using it. Now that you have obtained a copy of a compression utility, such as Stuffit Expander or Stuffit Lite, using helper applications is much easier.

To view additional graphic file formats, you're going to use a helper application called JPEGView. Don't be fooled. Despite its name, JPEGView displays a variety of graphics types such as JPEG, PICT, GIF, TIFF, BMP, and MacPaint.

There are numerous FTP sites where you can find this program. However, I'll save you the trouble of looking. The following site not only provides you with a copy of JPEGView, but offers many additional applications that you can use, some of which you'll get in upcoming lessons.

1. Using your preferred method, go to **ftp://ftp.ncsa.uiuc.edu/Mac/Mosaic/Helpers/**.
2. Scroll down until you see jpegview3.31.sit.hqx. Click it and wait for it to download on your machine. Remember from Lesson 15 that you need another helper application, such as Stuffit Expander, to decompress this program.

Is That All I Need? JPEGView is probably all you'll need for just about any graphic you may find on the Web. However, two more applications, GraphicConverter and GIFConverter, are also excellent. As long as you're there, you might consider downloading them, too. They are listed as **gifconverter-237.hqx** and **graphic-converter213.hqx**. Of course, as new releases come out, the numbers will change, but the basic names will remain the same.

3. Place the JPEGView folder anywhere you'd like and return to Netscape. Many people like to create a Graphics folder in which they keep all of their graphic files and applications.

Using JPEGView as a Helper

Now that you have your copy of JPEGView installed, you must let Netscape know how to use it as a helper application. Because Netscape automatically views JPEG and GIF images, you'll set Netscape to view bitmap (BMP) images.

1. In Netscape, open the Options menu and choose Preferences. The Preferences dialog box appears.
2. From the pop-up menu at the top of the Preferences dialog box, choose Helper Applications.
3. Click the New button for the new setting.
4. A new dialog box appears. Click in the **Mime Type** field and type **image**.
5. Click in the **Mime Subtype** field and type **bmp**. Your dialog box should look like Figure 19.1. Click the OK button.

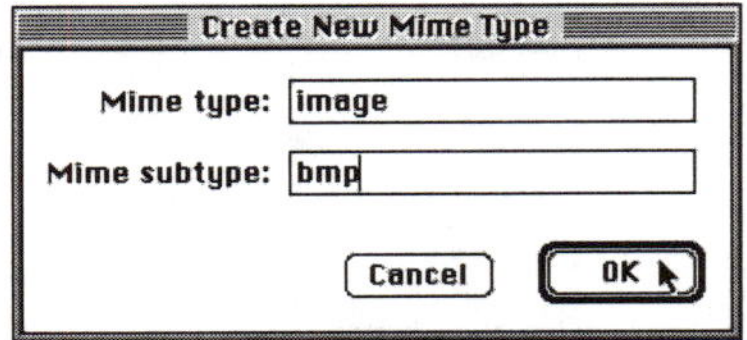

FIGURE 19.1 The Create New Mime Type dialog box.

6. When you return to the Preferences dialog box, click in the **Extensions** field and type **bmp**.
7. Click the Browse button next to **Application: Unknown**. In this dialog box, find and then choose JPEGView.
8. Now select the Launch Application radio button next to **Action**. When you have done this, your dialog box should look like Figure 19.2. Click the OK button and you're done.

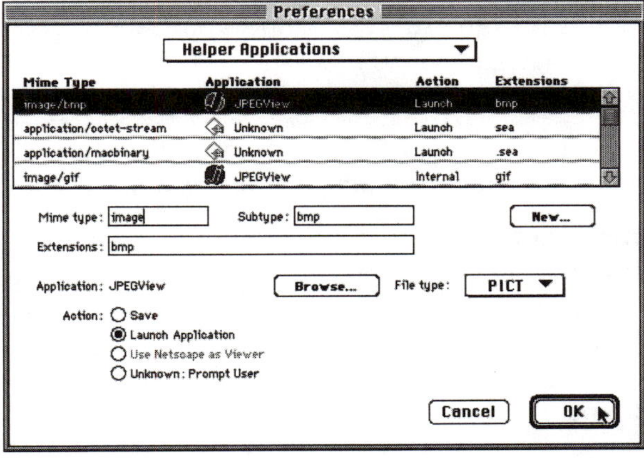

FIGURE 19.2 The completed Helper Applications dialog box.

To see how a helper application works with graphics, you'll need to download a bitmap to test:

1. Using your preferred method, go to **http://dunkin.Princeton.edu/.golf/images/bmps/master.bmp**.
2. Wait for Netscape to download the file. When it does, JPEGView should launch and you should see a picture of the 12th hole at Augusta National—home of The Master's PGA golf tournament (see Figure 19.3).

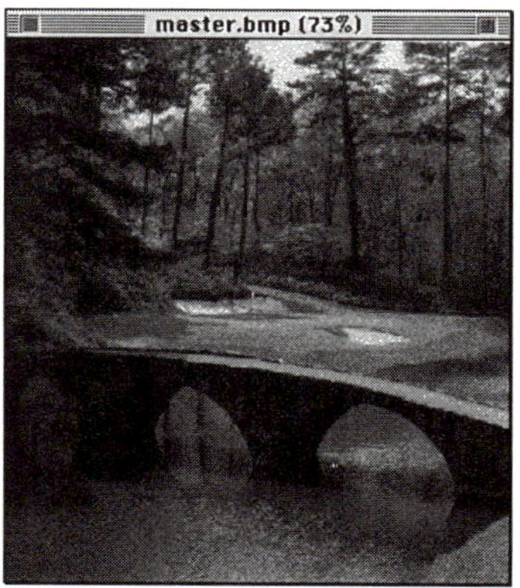

FIGURE 19.3 JPEGView displays a bitmap.

Watch That Size! Try to find the size of an image before downloading it for display. Some decompressed image types, such as bitmaps and TIFFs, can be quite large and can take a long time to download. If you have a slow connection, you may not want to take the time to do this.

SAVING GRAPHIC FILES

Although Netscape does display JPEGs and GIFs without a helper application, you can also set Netscape to use JPEGView for these, especially if you want to save or edit images. Most users choose not to, but the option is there if you want it. One advantage to using a helper application is that the file containing the image is actually saved on your computer when it is downloaded.

But what if you choose to let Netscape display JPEGs and GIFs without a helper application, and you still wish to save a copy on your computer? Fortunately, Netscape has made it very easy to do so. Here's how:

1. Click the link representing the graphic file you want to save and hold down your mouse button for a couple of seconds. When you do, a pop-up menu, such as the one pictured in Figure 19.4, is displayed.

FIGURE 19.4 A pop-up menu that lets you Save this Image as...

2. Choose the Save this Image as option.
3. A dialog box appears in which you can name and save the image to the location you prefer (most people use the name and location Netscape suggests, but feel free to change it). Click the Save button, and you're done.

In this lesson, you learned how to configure Netscape to use a helper application to view various types of graphic files. In the next lesson, you learn how to use Netscape to play sound files.

Playing Sound Using Netscape

In this lesson, you learn how to configure Netscape to play audio clips found on the Web.

What Are Audio Files?

In respect to how long it takes to download, sound files fall somewhere between still pictures and full-motion video (which you'll learn about in the next lesson). Many sound files are small enough to download in a short amount of time and interesting enough to be worth it.

Having said that, however, be assured that there are a lot of very large sound files out there on the Web that can take significant time to download. This is one similarity between sound and graphic files. Some are big, some are small. Some are worth downloading, some aren't. As always, make sure you really want to listen to a file if it is very large.

Another similarity between sound and graphic files is that there are many different formats out there. Unlike graphics, Netscape won't play any sound files without a helper application, so you'll need one that will play as many types of files as possible. The most popular audio file formats on the Web are:

- **Sun Audio** Sun Audio is perhaps the most popular sound format on the Web. Sun Audio files generally have an AU file extension.

- **WAVE** A close second, and perhaps gaining on Sun Audio, is the WAVE format. The WAVE (WAV) standard was developed and standardized on the IBM PC platform. One problem with WAVE files is their extreme variability in file type, although a good helper application can generally take care of this.
- **AIFF** The Audio Interchange File Format is a Macintosh standard generally used for large files. AIFF files are a distant third to WAVE and AU files, but they are out there nonetheless.

There are, of course, other formats, but these three comprise the most popular found on the Web.

Configuring Netscape for Sound

As already mentioned, you'll need a helper application to listen to audio files downloaded from the Web. One of the most flexible applications around is SoundApp by Norman Franke. It plays close to a dozen different sound formats.

To get this file, you're going to abandon the NCSA site for a bit and go to another site. To get SoundApp:

1. Using your preferred method, go to **ftp://romulus.ucs.uoknor.edu:/mirrors/mac/sound/soundutil/**.
2. Find soundapp1.5.cpt.hqx and click it. Once again, the file will be decompressed by Stuffit Expander or another utility.
3. After it has been downloaded and decompressed, place it in a desired location on your Macintosh.

This Isn't SoundMachine! You may have heard that many people use SoundMachine as their audio player. However, with the proliferation of WAVE formats (a format SoundMachine doesn't fully support), SoundApp might be the better choice. If you would like to have Sound-Machine as well, go to back to our familiar site and get **ftp://ftp.ncsa.uiuc.edu/Mac/ Mosaic/Helpers/ sound-machine-21.hqx**.

As with JPEGView, you must tell Netscape that SoundApp is there and how to use it. To do so:

1. Open the Options menu and choose Preferences. The Preferences dialog box appears.
2. From the pop-up menu at the top of the Preferences dialog box, select Helper Applications.
3. Click the New button for the new setting.
4. A new dialog box appears. Click in the **Mime** field and type **audio**.
5. Click in the **Mime Subtype** field and type **x-wav**. Then click the OK button.
6. When you return to the Preferences dialog box, click in the **Extensions** field and type **wav**.
7. Click the Browse button next to **Application: Unknown**. In this dialog box, find and then choose SoundApp.
8. Now select the Launch Application radio button next to **Action**. When you have done this, your dialog box should look like Figure 20.1.

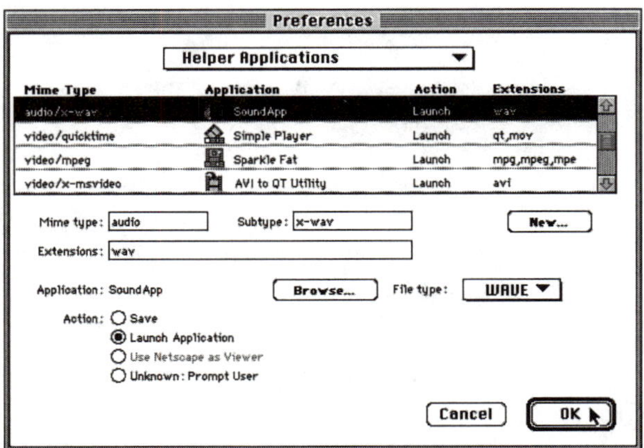

FIGURE 20.1 The completed Helper Applications Preferences dialog box.

9. Click the OK button and you're done.

Configure the Rest As mentioned earlier, there are quite a few sound file types competing for your attention. As long as you're configuring for sound, you might as well tell Netscape how to handle the other popular formats. To do so, complete Steps 1-9 above. However:

- For AU files, enter **basic** and **au,snd** in Steps 5 and 6 respectively.
- For AIFF files, enter **aiff** and **aiff,aif** in Steps 5 and 6 respectively.

TESTING YOUR HELPER APPLICATION

To make sure everything works, you need to test your new helper application. To do so, let's visit a Web page with lots of sound files:

1. Using your preferred method, go to **http://ai.eecs.umich.edu/people/kennyp/sounds.html**. This page has hundreds of sound files for just about every TV show you can imagine. You can scroll down through all of the links, or you can use the Find button. A sample of just a few of the theme songs available is shown in Figure 20.2.

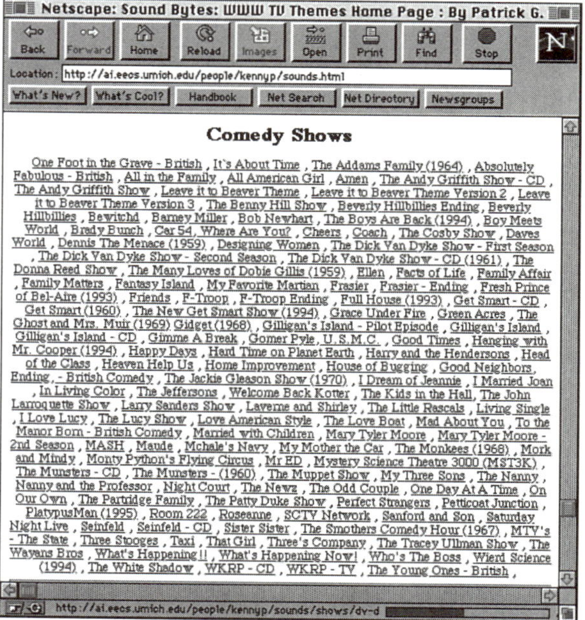

FIGURE 20.2 TV show theme links.

2. Using the Find button, search for **Frasier**. This takes you to the theme song of the TV show "Frasier." Of course, if you'd like to find another show of your choice, feel free.

3. Click the Frasier link. The file will be downloaded to your machine and automatically played.

As with graphics and sound files, Netscape has saved this file on your computer. You can now save it, use it, or trash it.

One handy feature of SoundApp is its ability to convert most popular sound formats into System 7 sounds. Once converted, you just click the icon representing a sound and it plays without any external applications. To do this:

1. In SoundApp, open the File menu and choose the Convert option.
2. Then, choose System 7 Sound in the **Convert To** pop-up menu, double-click the sound you want to convert, and you're done (see Figure 20.3).

FIGURE 20.3 Converting sound using SoundApp.

In this lesson, you learned how to configure Netscape to play sound files. In the next lesson, you learn how to configure Netscape to play full-motion video clips.

Playing Full-Motion Video

LESSON 21

In this lesson, you learn how to configure Netscape to play full-motion video clips obtained from the Web.

What Is Full-Motion Video?

The vast majority of the graphics you'll currently find on the Web are still images. However, the emergence of full-motion video has come about as Web authors begin to discover new uses for this medium.

Web Authors Keep in mind that each Web page you see is a file that somebody had to create and get ready for you to look at. The person who does this is often referred to as a Web author. You will also see this person referred to as a Web master or Web programmer, among other things.

The reason that full-motion video hasn't yet become a real force on the Web is simple—size. Full-motion video files tend to be very large. Because you must download these Web files before viewing them, you should have a very fast connection in order to make viewing video clips worth your time.

For most people using a high-speed Network connection to surf the Web, this generally isn't a problem. However, a large portion of those on the Net are using standard 14.4 or 28.8 modems. For these people, even a relatively small video clip can take 5 to 10 minutes to download and view.

However, as new technologies become available, this problem will begin to slowly disappear. There are already signs of this happening. In East Lansing, Michigan, for instance, a local cable company is offering full Internet connections through its standard cable service. This means residents can watch Gilligan's Island reruns at the same time they read their e-mail! There is no doubt that these technologies will continue to proliferate, making data available faster and more reliable in the future.

Configuring Netscape for Full-Motion Video

If you're willing to wait a few minutes, though, you can view full-motion video with relative ease. However, Netscape needs yet another helper application to display these full-motion video files, called *MPEGs*.

MPEG MPEG, which stands for Moving Pictures Experts Group, has become the standard format for digitized full-motion video. New, better, and different standards—such as MPEG2, AVI, and others—are emerging all the time, but most of the files you'll find on the Web are MPEG. By the way, if you want to learn more than you've ever wanted to know about MPEG, take a peek at **http://www.cs.tu-berlin.de/~phade/mpegfaq/index.html**.

The standard helper application for viewing MPEGs on the Macintosh is called Sparkle. To get this file, let's go back to the familiar FTP site at **ftp://ftp.ncsa.uiuc.edu/Mac/Mosaic/Helpers/**. Sparkle is listed as **sparkle-242.hqx**.

I Need To Upgrade! Sparkle is only fully supported under Macintosh System 7.5. If you're using System 7.0 or 7.1, you should get a copy of MPEG Player 0.3. This program isn't nearly as nice as Sparkle, but it will play MPEGs in a pinch. It can be found at **ftp://ftp.sunet.se// pub/mac/info-mac/app/mac-mpeg-030.hqx**.

Simply click sparkle-242.hqx to download it to your computer. This also might be a good time to take a break and stretch your legs—Sparkle is quite a large application; it can take 5 to 10 minutes to download.

As you did with the other two helper applications, wait for Stuffit Expander to decompress Sparkle. Once it has been downloaded, place it anywhere you'd like on your computer. After you have Sparkle installed, you must show Netscape how to use it:

1. Open the Options menu and choose Preferences. The Preferences dialog box appears.
2. From the pop-up menu at the top of the Preferences dialog box, choose Helper Applications.
3. Click the New button for the new setting.
4. A new dialog box appears. Click in the **Mime Type** field and type **video**.
5. Click in the **Mime Subtype** field and type **mpeg**. Click the OK button.
6. When you return to the Preferences dialog box, click in the **Extensions** field and type **mpg,mpeg,mpe**.
7. Click the Browse button next to **Application: Unknown**. In this dialog box, find and then choose Sparkle (or Sparkle Fat if you're using a Power Macintosh).
8. Now select the Launch Application radio button next to **Action**. When you have done this, your dialog box should look like Figure 21.1. Click the OK button and you're done.

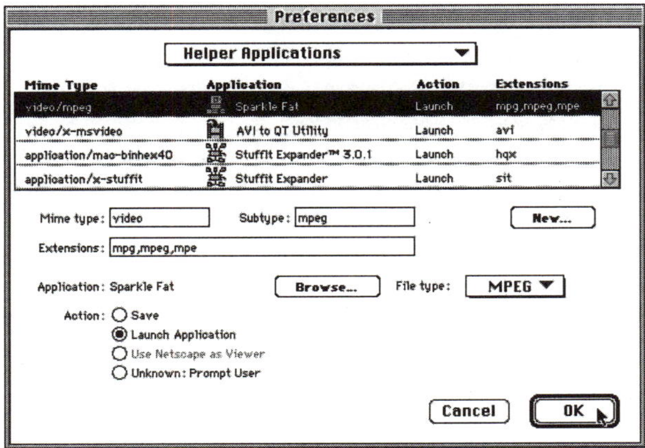

FIGURE 21.1 The completed Helper Applications dialog box.

PLAYING FULL-MOTION VIDEO FILES

Now to test your newly installed helper application, let's go to a Web site that has MPEG full-motion video files you can play:

1. Using your preferred method, go to **http://www.cnam.fr/fractals/anim.html**.
2. This page has quite a few movies. Scroll down until you see a group of movies. Pick the MPEG link under the description **Fast fly through of a fractal-generated landscape** (see Figure 21.2).

Before Christmas, Please! Remember, I said earlier that full-motion video files tend to be quite large. Try to pick smaller ones, and if you do pick a large one, make sure it's one you really want to look at!

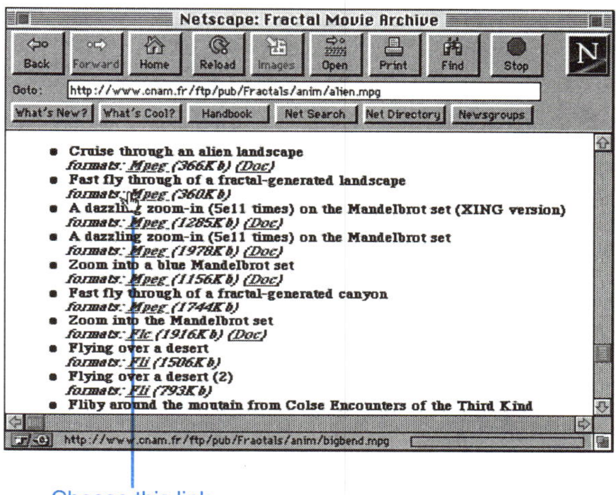

FIGURE 21.2 Fly through a fractal-generated landscape.

3. When the file is downloaded, Netscape launches Sparkle and plays the video.

As with graphics and sound files, Netscape has saved this file on your computer. You can save it, use it, or trash it.

A Quicker Movie A very attractive feature of Sparkle is its ability to convert MPEGs to QuickTime video. While your MPEG is still open, open the File menu and choose Save As. Save it as a QuickTime movie, accept the default settings Sparkle recommends for saving, and click OK. When Sparkle is finished converting the file, you have a movie that can be instantly imported into many Macintosh applications. Just make sure you have plenty of disk space!

In this lesson, you learned how to configure Netscape to play full-motion video files. In the next lesson, you learn how to do some shopping on the Internet.

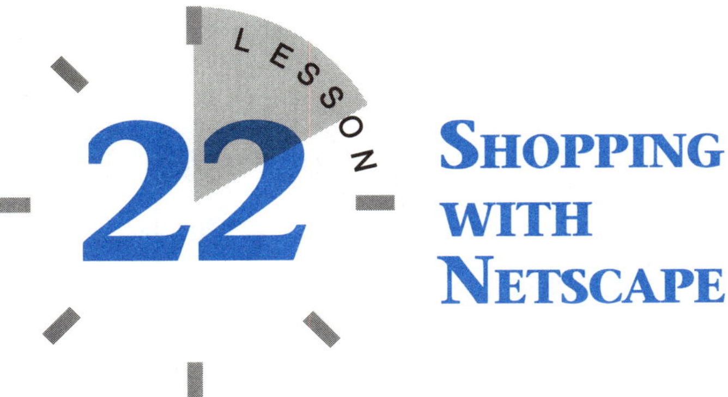

Shopping with Netscape

In this lesson, you learn how to use Netscape to shop on the Internet.

Shopping the Internet

The Internet was originally designed as a way for university and government agencies to transmit information for nonprofit use. In recent years, however, the Internet has expanded to include a variety of additional services.

One area that is undergoing considerable growth is the commercial sector. To coin a phrase, "business is booming." The number and range of businesses getting on the Internet are growing almost as fast as the Internet itself.

Presently, there are dozens of shopping outlets available on the Internet. Many give you online catalogs to browse, and many are happy to take your orders online.

Security Concerns! Despite the assurances of many shopping outlets on the Internet that their transactions are secure, many security experts believe that these transactions are not 100% secure, and might still be open to unauthorized access. Before you give out a credit card number or password to an online shopping service, be aware that the potential still exists, no matter how small, for that information to reach someone other than the intended recipient. Some of the sites you'll look at in this lesson don't require this information, however.

Locating Online Shopping Outlets

One of the best ways to locate shopping outlets on the Internet is to use the Yahoo Web page database (described in Lesson 10) to search on the keyword "shopping."

A Yahoo search turned up 247 places to shop. No doubt by the time you read this, the number will be even higher. A sample of some of the Internet shopping malls is shown in Figure 22.1.

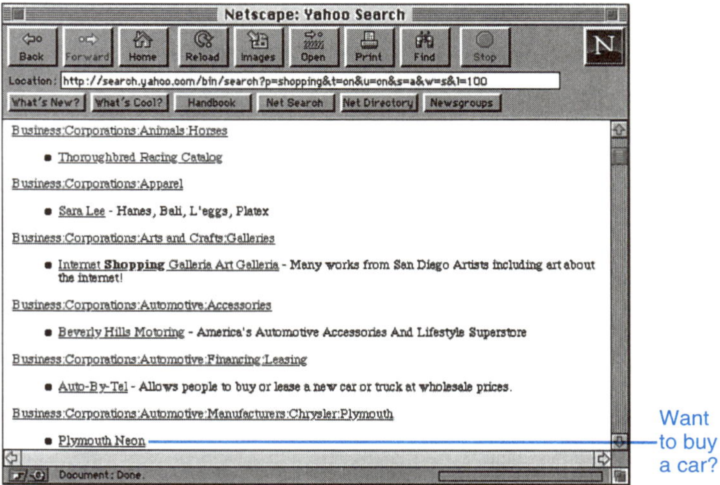

Figure 22.1 Places to shop on the Internet.

Because it's impossible to cover all of the major shopping outlets available on the Internet, we're going to look at one of the biggest—Shopping 2000. While there, you're going to have an opportunity to get a free issue of *The Net* Internet magazine. There is also a list of additional sites at the end of this lesson.

From the Yahoo search results page:

1. Scroll down until you find the Shopping 2000 link and click. This takes you to its home page (see Figure 22.2).

FIGURE 22.2 Shopping 2000.

2. Click the Music, Books, Video & Art link.
3. Scroll down until you see the Free Offer Forum link and click it. This takes you to its home page.
4. From there, if you scroll down, you will see a number of links (see Figure 22.3). Click the Browse by Category link.

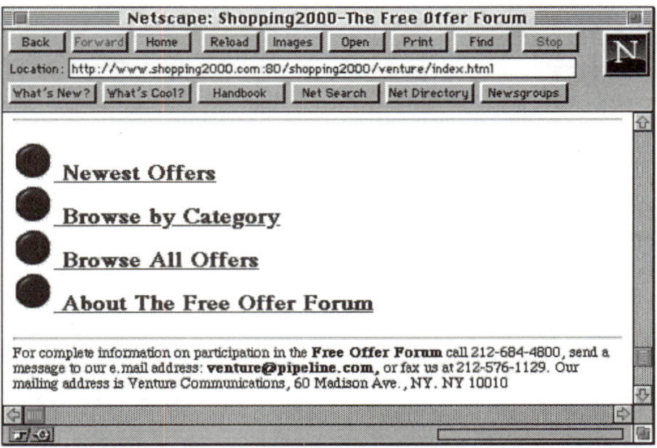

FIGURE 22.3 Choosing your free offer by category.

5. Scroll down and locate the Computers link and click it.
6. There are a number of offers on this Web page. Find and click The Net link.

7. You are now on *The Net*'s free issue order page. Scroll down until the order form is displayed. Complete the requested information (it does not ask for a credit card number!) so that your screen looks like Figure 22.4.

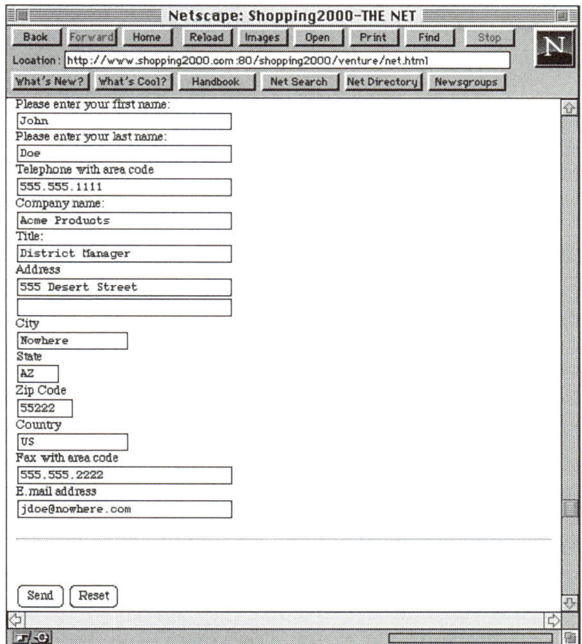

FIGURE 22.4 A completed order form.

8. If you wish to receive a free issue of this magazine, click the Send button. Your information will be given to *The Net* and you should receive your free trial issue in several weeks.

Most of the shopping you do on the Net will be similar to the above process. You'll locate something you want and then you'll place an order for it. Sometimes you'll be referred to an 800 number; other times you'll be asked for a credit card or other information.

As promised, here are some other popular shopping sites:

- **Upper Deck Authenticated** Part of Shopping 2000, this is a warehouse of sports memorabilia. Last time I checked, it was offering a Mickey Mantle baseball. It can be located at **http://www.shopping2000.com/shopping2000/upperdeck/**.
- **San Francisco Music Box** Yet another store at Shopping 2000. If it makes music (and sometimes even if it doesn't), you can find it at **http:/www.shopping2000.com/shopping2000/music_box/**.
- **Global Shopping Network** They boast over 100,000 products available. They offer other services too. Find them at **http://www.gsn.com/**.
- **Internet Shopping Mall in Thailand** When you're really ready to go around the world, visit this site. In addition to shopping, find tourist information on the best hotels in Thailand and more. They are located at **http://goldsite.com/**.
- **Macintosh Shopping Directory** If you can actually type in the entire URL for this site, you'll be well-rewarded. Everything under the sun for Macintosh computers can be found at **http://www.wincorp.com/windata/OneWorldPlaza/WINMacShoppingDirectory/WINMacShoppingDirectory.html**

In this lesson, you learned how to use Netscape to shop online on the Internet. In the next lesson, you learn how to make Netscape look like *you* want it to.

Customizing Netscape's Appearance

In this lesson, you learn how to customize Netscape's appearance so it looks like you want it to.

Displaying More of Your Netscape Screen

Everyone wants to see more of what's there to see—Web pages. As you can tell, the toolbar, directory buttons, and Location field take up a significant amount of room on the Netscape window. These elements can be altered or removed to give you more room for viewing actual Web pages.

Altering the Toolbar

The nine icons that make up Netscape's toolbar are simply shortcuts to commands that appear on the File, Edit, View, and Go menus (they're also available via keyboard shortcuts).

You can do two things to the toolbar to increase your viewing area. First, you can alter the toolbar button's appearance to make more room. To do this:

1. Open the Options menu and choose the Preferences option.
2. In the Preferences dialog box, choose the Windows and Link Styles option.
3. The **Show toolbar as** option has three radio buttons next to it. Netscape's default is to show the toolbar buttons as both Pictures and text. You can click either Text or Pictures. Clicking Text reduces the size the most and makes your Netscape screen look like Figure 23.1.

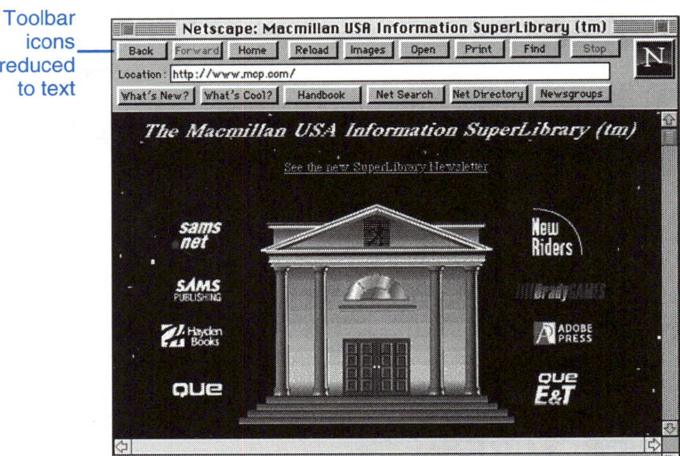

FIGURE 23.1 Toolbar buttons as text.

But there is yet another option—removing the toolbar altogether. This is also easily accomplished:

1. Open the Options menu.
2. Under that menu are a number of choices. Click the Show Toolbar option so that there is no longer a check mark next to it. This makes the toolbar buttons disappear.

They're Baaaaack! You removed the toolbar buttons, but the next time you use Netscape, they're back again. Don't worry, just make sure that you choose the Save Options item under the Options menu before you quit Netscape.

REMOVING THE LOCATION FIELD

The Location field displays the URL of the current page or file you are viewing. This information is very helpful. However, if you feel that viewing more screen area is more important than seeing the URL, you can remove it.

1. Open the Options menu.
2. Click the Show Location item to remove the check mark. The Location field is no longer displayed.

REMOVING THE DIRECTORY BUTTONS

For maximum viewing area, there is one more thing you can eliminate: the directory buttons. As with the toolbar buttons, the corresponding commands are available in the Directory and Help menus:

1. Open the Options menu.
2. Click the Show Directory Buttons item to remove the check mark. The directory buttons are no longer displayed.

With the toolbar buttons, Location field, and directory buttons removed, much more of your screen can now be viewed. Figure 23.2 shows how Netscape looks with all of these options turned off.

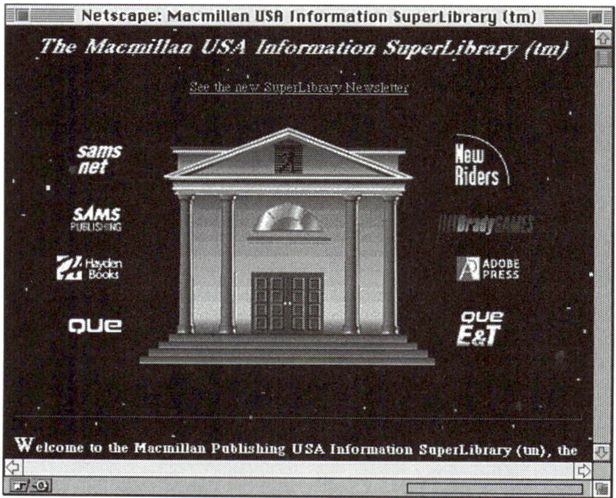

FIGURE 23.2 Netscape with no clickable options.

CHANGING THE FONT

There is one more way to increase your viewing area that many people don't think about. You can change the font size that Netscape displays. Netscape sets the *proportional* and *fixed fonts* to Times 12 and Courier 10 respectively.

Proportional and Fixed Fonts There are basically two font types. Proportional fonts, such as Times, allow for different characters to take up a different amount of space (or pixels) on-screen. For instance, an *o* takes up more space than an *i*. A fixed font, such as Courier, on the other hand, means that each character on the screen takes up exactly the same amount of space.

Changing these fonts is easy, although it might require some experimentation on your part to find a combination that fits your tastes.

1. Open the Options menu and choose the Preferences option.
2. In the Preferences dialog box, choose the Fonts and Colors option so that your screen looks like that pictured in Figure 23.3.

   The settings you are concerned with are the **Use the Proportional Font**, **Use the Fixed Font**, and **Size**. It is recommended that you keep Courier as your fixed font, but the proportional font and both font's sizes are up to you.
3. To change the font, click the desired font pop-up menu and choose the desired font.
4. To change the font size, click the desired font size pop-up menu and choose the desired size.
5. Click the OK button when you're done. The changes are immediately reflected in the Netscape window.

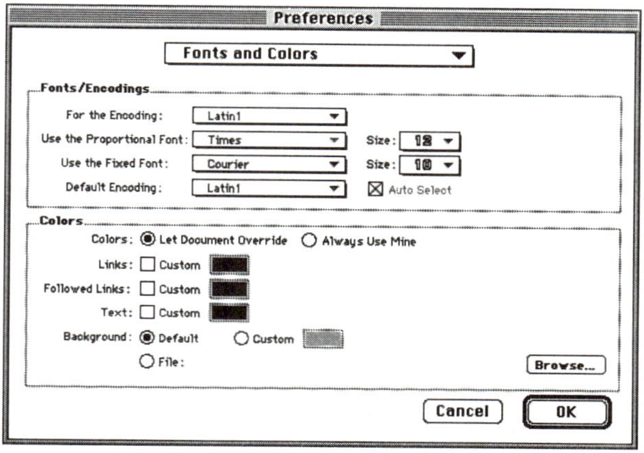

Figure 23.3 The Fonts and Colors Preferences dialog box.

This greatly effects the amount of information that can be displayed in Netscape. Figures 23.4 and 23.5 show the difference between Proportional Font Times 12/Fixed Font Courier 10 and Proportional Font Times 10/Fixed Font Courier 9.

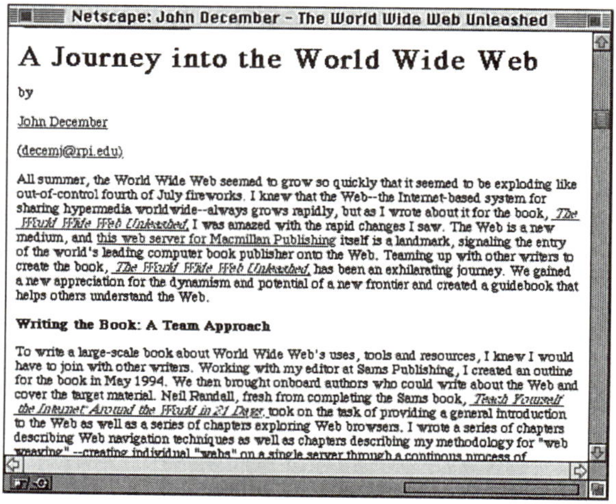

Figure 23.4 Proportional Font Times 12/Fixed Font Courier 10.

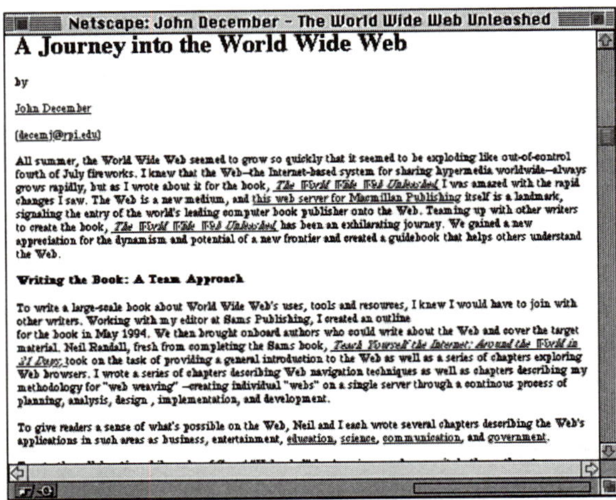

FIGURE 23.5 Proportional Font Times 10/Fixed Font Courier 9.

CHANGING COLORS

One thing most users eventually get tired of is seeing the same screen colors day in and day out. Perhaps you'd like some say in what color Netscape displays, or maybe you'd even like a picture as Netscape's background.

To set your own colors:

1. Open the Options menu and choose the Preferences option.
2. In the Preferences dialog box, choose the Fonts and Colors option, as you did in the last section.
3. To change Links, Followed Links, or Text color, simply select the check box next to each option, and then click the colored box next to that option. You can then choose your own color from a dialog box like that shown in Figure 23.6.

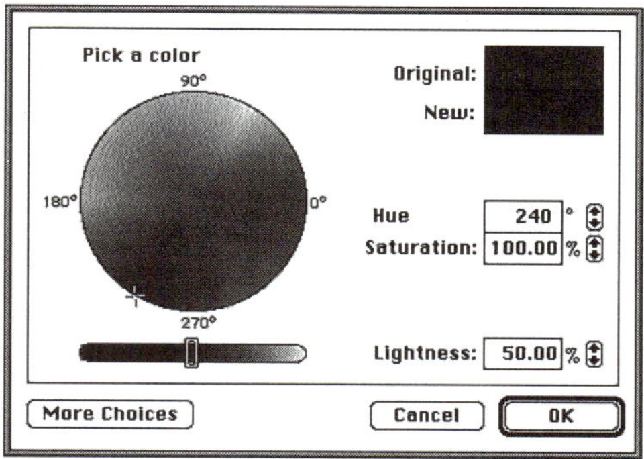

FIGURE 23.6 The Custom Color selection dialog box.

4. If you want to change the Background color, simply select the Custom radio button, click the colored box next to that option, and proceed as you did in Step 3.

If you prefer, you can even use a GIF or JPEG as your window background. Simply select the File radio button, and then click the Browse button to select the picture you'd like to use.

If you want to always view the nifty graphics and colors that certain Web pages have, make sure the Let Document Override radio button is selected, as seen in Figure 23.3.

In this lesson, you learned how to change Netscape's screen appearance. In the next lesson, you learn how to set some of Netscape's important configurations.

Configuring Netscape

In this lesson, you learn how to make more advanced configuration changes in Netscape.

Changing Netscape's Configuration Options

If you want to learn how to tailor Netscape to suit your needs and tastes even more than you did in the last lesson, this lesson is a must-read. In fact, depending on how you are connected to the Internet, you might find that you *have* to change some configurations in order for Netscape to work correctly.

If you're running Netscape on a computer attached to a *LAN*, there's a good chance your system administrator has already made all of the necessary configuration changes you'll need. If you are running Netscape on a LAN, make sure you consult your system administrator before you make any further changes in your configuration. If you're running Netscape on a Macintosh that dials in to the Internet using a modem, it's up to you to make sure you have Netscape configured properly.

LAN A Local Area Network is simply a group of computers connected together in one location so that certain resources—such as files, hard disk space, printers, and other external devices and services—can be shared.

All of the configuration settings in this lesson are made in Netscape's Preferences dialog box. Remember that you can get to these settings by opening the Options menu and choosing the Preferences option.

STYLES

Choosing the Window and Link Styles option from the pop-up menu in the Preferences dialog box allows you to configure certain aspects of Netscape's appearance. In the last lesson, you learned how to set the appearance of Netscape's toolbar.

Some other configurations you can set from this dialog box:

- **Start with** This allows you to tell Netscape whether to display a blank page or a particular URL at start-up.
- **Underline links** If you select this check box, Netscape underlines all links in addition to displaying them in a different color. If you do not select this check box, links are not underlined.
- **Followed Links Expire** This configuration tells Netscape how long to keep a link you've followed displayed as a different color. You cannot set this link for less than 1 day. You can also tell Netscape to expire all of the followed links immediately by clicking the Now button.

All of the changes in this dialog box are cosmetic and have no real effect on how Netscape operates. Feel free to set them according to your personal preferences.

FONTS AND COLORS

The Fonts and Colors option, which was covered in detail in the last lesson, contains settings that deal with Netscape's appearance. Again, you can experiment with these to find settings that suit your personal preferences.

The only settings that weren't discussed were the Encoding options. These settings have to do with the characters Netscape is displayed in and uses. There are two types of characters: Latin (alphabet) or Japanese (character). You will want to keep these configurations set to Latin1.

MAIL AND NEWS

The settings for Netscape's Mail and News options were covered in Lesson 16. However, there were a couple of settings that weren't covered: Signature File and Send and Post. Let's take a look at those now.

Signature A signature is a way of identifying yourself on the Net. Typically, signatures contain your name, e-mail address, and any other identifying information you choose to include. They also often contain a short saying that you might like. One thing you should do is keep your signature short—under 5 lines is typical.

The first configuration to look at is the Signature File setting. Creating and using a signature file is easy:

1. Open a new document in a simple word processor. It's recommended that you use SimpleText or TeachText for this exercise.
2. Type in your desired signature and save it under an appropriate name, such as **signature**. A typical signature is pictured in Figure 24.1. Once created, you can also use this signature file with other applications, such as Eudora.
3. When you return to the Netscape Preferences dialog box, click File next to **Signature File**.
4. Click the Browse button to locate the file you just created. Double-click it to return to the Preferences dialog box with your signature file selected.

```
signature
Noel Estabrook - MSU              |    There are three types of people in this
Instructional Design & Tech --|--  world, those who can count, and those
514B Erickson Hall                |    who cannot.
noele@msu.edu                     |
```

Figure 24.1 A typical signature composed in SimpleText.

The Send and Post setting is one that you shouldn't have to change. Remember when you configured helper applications? One of the settings was Mime Type. This is a way in which certain files are identified by extensions, such as HQX. You should leave this setting at Allow 8-bit.

Cache and Network

The settings for Netscape's caching options (see Figure 24.2) were mentioned in Lesson 5. It's now time to find out what to do with them.

Caching Caching is nothing more than a computer's way of temporarily storing data so that the data doesn't take up precious RAM, which increases Netscape's speed as well. The higher number your disk cache is, the more information Netscape can temporarily store. However, because data is cached to your hard drive, make sure you have enough hard disk space available.

Because your Cache Directory is automatically set by Netscape, you will not have to change this setting. However, you can adjust your Cache Size. Simply click the up or down arrow to change this setting.

Netscape tells you how much space you have available for cache. In Figure 24.2, for example, the user has set cache to approximately 10% of available disk space. Of course, you can clear out the disk cache at any time by clicking the Clear Disk Cache Now button.

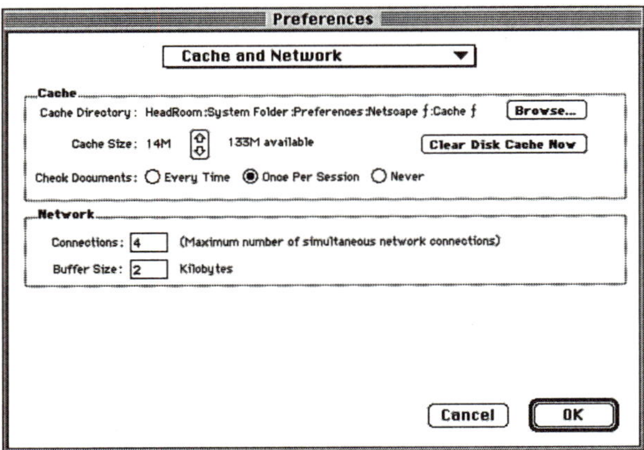

FIGURE 24.2 The Cache and Network Preferences dialog box.

The Check Documents setting determines how often you have Netscape attempt to download a page. For instance, let's assume you go to **http://www.mcp.com/**. Once you leave that page, Netscape stores the information that was contained on that page in cache. That way, if you go back to that page during your session, Netscape doesn't need to bother downloading the page again; it just gets the information from cache.

That's where this setting comes in. If you configure this setting to Every Time, Netscape will never check cache for a document. If you choose Once Per Session (the recommended setting), Netscape will download the data once and then use cache from then on. If you choose Never, Netscape will always try to read a document from cache.

The settings for network connections should only be a concern if you're operating Netscape on a LAN. If you are on a LAN, consult your system administrator before changing either of the network settings.

IMAGES AND SECURITY

The Images and Security settings (see Figure 24.3) deal with two areas. First, the Images setting determines how images are displayed on your screen. Second, the Security settings tell Netscape what actions should be taken to alert you when you encounter insecure information on the Web.

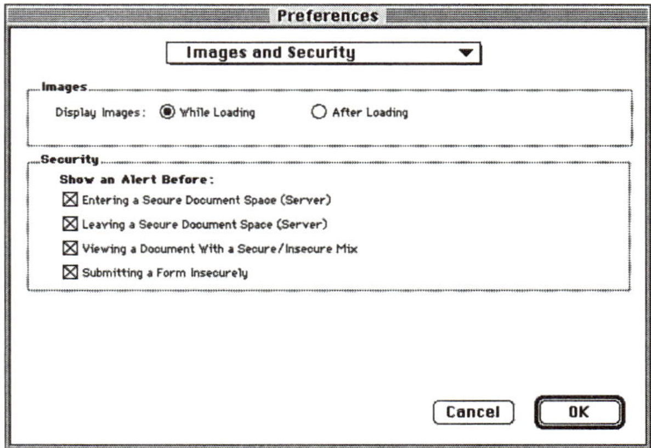

FIGURE 24.3 The Images and Security Preferences dialog box.

If you configure the Display Images setting to While Loading, Netscape will display partial images at the same time it loads text. This is the preferred method because you can begin reading Web text even before images are completely downloaded. However, if you want Netscape to wait to display graphics until they're fully loaded, choose the After Loading option.

As was mentioned in Lesson 22, some information on the Web is not fully secure. Whether you wish to be warned of the security status of a particular Web resource is up to you. If you do, select the box next to the resource. If not, leave the boxes empty.

APPLICATIONS AND DIRECTORIES

If you recall, the Directories setting was covered in Lesson 15. However, the Supporting Applications area has not yet been covered, so let's talk about that now.

A *supporting application* is identical to the helper applications you have seen throughout this book. These are applications that help Netscape communicate with different parts of the Internet. For instance, Lesson 13 mentioned Telnet sessions. In order for Netscape to conduct a Telnet session, it must have an external application to do so.

To set these configurations, simply click the corresponding Browse button and select the application you want to use. Here's a list of recommended applications (and where you can get them):

- **Telnet Application** This setting configures Netscape to conduct a standard Telnet session. You can use Telnet 2.7, which can be found at **ftp://ftp.ncsa.uiuc.edu/Telnet/Mac/Telnet2.7/**.
- **TN3270 Application** Allows you to configure Netscape to conduct an IBM 3270-type Telnet session. You can use TN3270_2.4a7, which can be found at **ftp://boombox.micro.umn.edu:/pub/gopher/Macintosh-TurboGopher/helper applications/TN3270_2.4a7.sea.hqx**.
- **View Source** This setting tells Netscape what application to use to view the HTML source code on a Web page. It is recommended that you use a simple word processor, such as SimpleText or TeachText. However, another good one to use would be BBEdit Lite, which can be found at **ftp://ftp.ncsa.uiuc.edu/Mac/Mosaic/Helpers/**.

PROXIES

If you are running Netscape on a stand-alone Macintosh, the settings under the Proxies Preference do not apply to you. They are used when your computer is connected to a LAN with a *firewall*. If you are on such a LAN, you should contact your system administrator to find out how to set these configurations.

Firewall? A firewall is a security measure taken to prevent unauthorized access to a local area network or an Internet server. As its name implies, a firewall provides a protective barrier that stops access to a given computer system.

HELPER APPLICATIONS

Netscape's Helper Applications settings have been covered in detail in Lesson 15 and Lessons 18-20. Please refer to those lessons for details on how to set helper applications.

In this lesson, you learned how to configure Netscape and set preferences for the options Netscape allows you to control.

Congratulations! You are now a certified Web surfer. You have all of the information you'll need to explore the World Wide Web with ease. But wait, don't put the *10 Minute Guide to Netscape for the Mac* on the shelf yet. Keep it near your computer to use as a fingertip reference whenever you have trouble remembering any of the commands and options covered in these lessons.

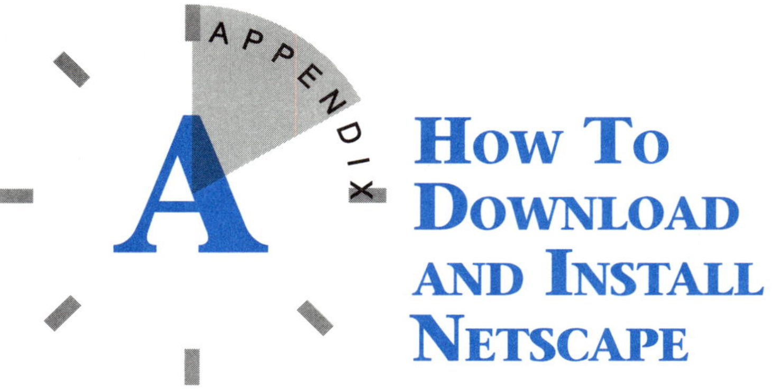

How To Download and Install Netscape

In this appendix, you learn how to download and install Netscape.

Since its first release, Netscape Navigator has been distributed as shareware from Netscape's FTP site. As a result, you must already have an Internet connection and an FTP client in order to get it. This appendix assumes you are able to get Netscape Navigator via FTP. However, if you can't, you can contact Netscape for a copy at:

Netscape

(415) 528-2555 (7:00 a.m. to 5:00 p.m. PST)

sales@netscape.com

Shareware Shareware is software that is freely distributed for a nominal fee. Netscape is distributed as shareware to those who work for government or educational institutions.

Downloading Netscape

If you don't have a program for downloading files from FTP sites, you can probably get one from your Internet Service Provider. If your Internet access is provided through a Local Area Network, contact your system administrator to acquire the necessary software (Fetch and Anarchie are two good ones).

When you're ready to get Netscape Navigator, tell your FTP client to go to Netscape's FTP site at:

ftp://ftp.netscape.com/pub/netscape/mac/

From this directory, tell your FTP client to get **netscape-1.1N.hqx**. This is the current version of Netscape Navigator. If Netscape releases *beta,* or more current versions of Navigator, the **1.1N** may change.

Beta A beta release or beta version of a software product is one that is still under development and may still contain "bugs" or errors. Beta releases allow you to sample new features the manufacturer is adding to the next official release of the program.

It is a large file, so it may take a while to download. Because this file is encoded, you also need a utility, such as Stuffit Lite, to decode the file (see Lesson 15 for details on this program). If you already have such a utility on your computer, your FTP client automatically decodes the file.

Installing Netscape

Once the file has been decoded, you're left with a file called **Netscape 1.1N Installer.** To install it:

1. Double-click the Netscape 1.1N Installer icon.
2. When the Intro window appears, click Continue.
3. Next, the Netscape Installer dialog box appears (see Figure A.1). Click the Switch Disk or Select Folder button if you want to change the default location of Navigator's installation.
4. Finally, click the Install button; Netscape Navigator will install.

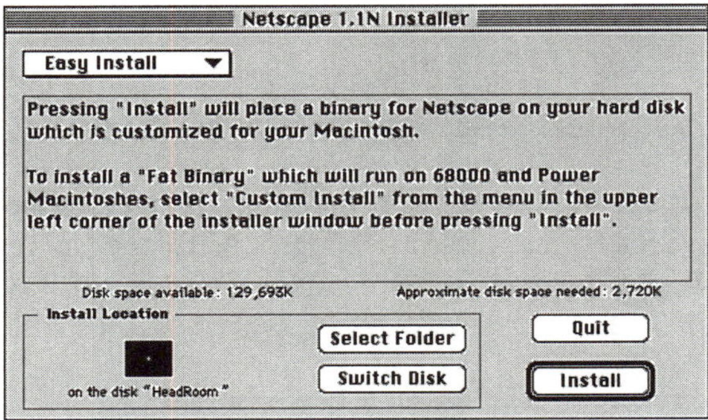

FIGURE A.1 The Netscape Installer dialog box.

If You're Fat If you have a Power Macintosh computer, you will want to install the version of Netscape Navigator that's designed to take advantage of this faster machine—what is referred to as a Fat file. Follow steps 1 through 3 above, but before continuing, click the pop-up menu and choose the Custom Install option. Next, select the Fat Binary option that you see in Figure A.2 and complete the installation.

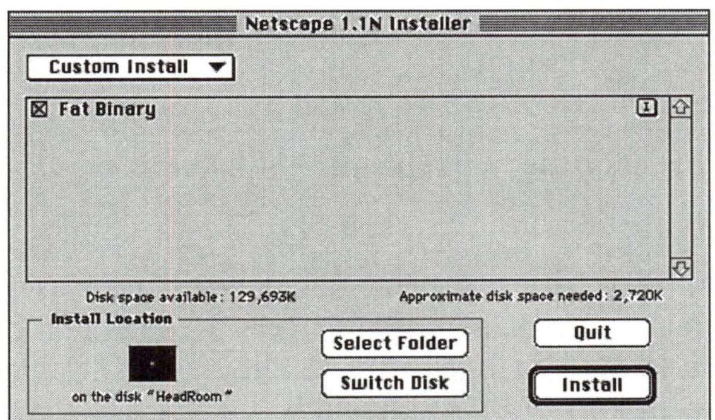

FIGURE A.2 Installing on a PowerMac.

The installer puts all of the necessary files where they belong. You are now ready to begin using Netscape Navigator.

INDEX

A

B

C

D

G

H

I

N

O

P

Q-R

S

T

U

Complete and Return this Card for a *FREE* Computer Book Catalog

Thank you for purchasing this book! You have purchased a superior computer book written expressly for your needs. To continue to provide the kind of up-to-date, pertinent coverage you've come to expect from us, we need to hear from you. Please take a minute to complete and return this self-addressed, postage-paid form. In return, we'll send you a free catalog of all our computer books on topics ranging from word processing to programming and the internet.

Mr. ☐ Mrs. ☐ Ms. ☐ Dr. ☐

Name (first) ☐☐☐☐☐☐☐☐☐☐☐ (M.I.) ☐ (last) ☐☐☐☐☐☐☐☐☐☐☐☐☐☐☐

Address ☐☐☐☐☐☐☐☐☐☐☐☐☐☐☐☐☐☐☐☐☐☐☐☐☐☐☐☐☐☐☐☐☐☐☐

☐☐☐☐☐☐☐☐☐☐☐☐☐☐☐☐☐☐☐☐☐☐☐☐☐☐☐☐☐☐☐☐☐☐☐

City ☐☐☐☐☐☐☐☐☐☐☐☐☐☐☐ State ☐☐ Zip ☐☐☐☐☐ ☐☐☐☐☐

Phone ☐☐☐ ☐☐☐ ☐☐☐☐ Fax ☐☐☐ ☐☐☐ ☐☐☐☐

Company Name ☐☐☐☐☐☐☐☐☐☐☐☐☐☐☐☐☐☐☐☐☐☐☐☐☐☐☐☐☐☐☐☐☐

E-mail address ☐☐☐☐☐☐☐☐☐☐☐☐☐☐☐☐☐☐☐☐☐☐☐☐☐☐☐☐☐☐☐☐☐

1. Please check at least (3) influencing factors for purchasing this book.

- Front or back cover information on book .... ☐
- Special approach to the content .... ☐
- Completeness of content .... ☐
- Author's reputation .... ☐
- Publisher's reputation .... ☐
- Book cover design or layout .... ☐
- Index or table of contents of book .... ☐
- Price of book .... ☐
- Special effects, graphics, illustrations .... ☐
- Other (Please specify): ______________ ☐

2. How did you first learn about this book?

- Internet Site .... ☐
- Saw in Macmillan Computer Publishing catalog .... ☐
- Recommended by store personnel .... ☐
- Saw the book on bookshelf at store .... ☐
- Recommended by a friend .... ☐
- Received advertisement in the mail .... ☐
- Saw an advertisement in: ______________ ☐
- Read book review in: ______________ ☐
- Other (Please specify): ______________ ☐

3. How many computer books have you purchased in the last six months?

This book only .... ☐ 3 to 5 books .... ☐
2 books .... ☐ More than 5 .... ☐

4. Where did you purchase this book?

- Bookstore .... ☐
- Computer Store .... ☐
- Consumer Electronics Store .... ☐
- Department Store .... ☐
- Office Club .... ☐
- Warehouse Club .... ☐
- Mail Order .... ☐
- Direct from Publisher .... ☐
- Internet site .... ☐
- Other (Please specify): .... ☐

5. How long have you been using a computer?

Less than 6 months .. ☐ 6 months to a year ..... ☐
1 to 3 years .... ☐ More than 3 years ...... ☐

6. What is your level of experience with personal computers and with the subject of this book?

	With PC's	With subject of book
New	☐	☐
Casual	☐	☐
Accomplished	☐	☐
Expert	☐	☐

Source Code — ISBN: 0-7897-0569-9

7. Which of the following best describes your job title?

- Administrative Assistant ☐
- Coordinator ☐
- Manager/Supervisor ☐
- Director ☐
- Vice President ☐
- President/CEO/COO ☐
- Lawyer/Doctor/Medical Professional ☐
- Teacher/Educator/Trainer ☐
- Engineer/Technician ☐
- Consultant ☐
- Not employed/Student/Retired ☐
- Other (Please specify): ☐

8. Which of the following best describes the area of the company your job title falls under?

- Accounting ☐
- Engineering ☐
- Manufacturing ☐
- Marketing ☐
- Operations ☐
- Sales ☐
- Other (Please specify): ☐

9. What is your age?

- Under 20 ☐
- 21-29 ☐
- 30-39 ☐
- 40-49 ☐
- 50-59 ☐
- 60-over ☐

10. Are you:

- Male ☐
- Female ☐

11. Which computer publications do you read regularly? (Please list)

____

____

____

____

____

____

____

____

____

Comments: ______________________________

____

____

Fold here and scotch-tape to ma

NO POSTAGE
NECESSARY
IF MAILED
IN THE
UNITED STATES

BUSINESS REPLY MAIL

FIRST-CLASS MAIL PERMIT NO. 9918 INDIANAPOLIS IN

POSTAGE WILL BE PAID BY THE ADDRESSEE

ATTN MARKETING
MACMILLAN COMPUTER PUBLISHING
MACMILLAN PUBLISHING USA
201 W 103RD ST
INDIANAPOLIS IN 46209-9042